Indigenous Storywork

Indigenous Storywork
Educating the Heart, Mind, Body, and Spirit

Jo-ann Archibald
Q'UM Q'UM XIIEM

UBCPress · Vancouver · Toronto

22 21 20 19 18 17 16   13 12 11 10 9 8

Printed in Canada on acid-free paper ∞

Library and Archives Canada Cataloguing in Publication

Archibald, Jo-ann, 1950-
    Indigenous storywork : educating the heart, mind, body, and spirit / Jo-Ann Archibald (Q'um Q'um Xiiem).

Includes bibliographical references and index.
ISBN 987-0-7748-1401-0 (bound); 978-0-7748-1402-7 (pbk.)

    1. Indians of North America – Canada – Folklore. 2. Storytelling – Canada. 3. Indians of North America – Education – Canada. I. Title.

E78.B9A73 2008   398.2089'97071   C2007-906656-9

Canadä

UBC Press gratefully acknowledges the financial support for our publishing program of the Government of Canada through the Book Publishing Industry Development Program (BPIDP), and of the Canada Council for the Arts, and the British Columbia Arts Council.

This book has been published with the help of the K.D. Srivastava Fund. We also gratefully acknowledge financial support from the BC Aboriginal Capacity and Developmental Research Environment (ACADRE) network.

Author royalties from this publication will be donated to the Coqualeetza Cultural Centre Elders' Group in Sardis, British Columbia, and the University of British Columbia Khot-La-Cha Student Award.

Printed and bound in Canada by Friesens
Set in Stone by Artegraphica Design Co. Ltd.
Copy editor: Robert Lewis
Proofreader: Sarah Munro
Indexer: David Luljak

UBC Press
The University of British Columbia
2029 West Mall
Vancouver, BC V6T 1Z2
604-822-5959 / Fax: 604-822-6083
www.ubcpress.ca

For my grandfather, Francis Kelly,

    who first showed me the value of learning

from Indigenous Elders

CONTENTS

PREFACE

First Nations/Indigenous stories about Coyote the Trickster often place her/him in a journeying mode, learning lessons the "hard" way. Trickster gets into trouble when she/he becomes disconnected from cultural traditional teachings. The Trickster stories remind us about the good power of interconnections within family, community, nation, culture, and land. If we become disconnected, we lose the ability to make meaning from Indigenous stories.

I took a long journey with Coyote the Trickster to learn about the "core" of Indigenous stories from Elders and to find a respectful place for stories and storytelling in education, especially in curricula. I also learned how to do story research with Elders. I worked intensively with three Coast Salish Elders and thirteen Stó:lō Elders who either were storytellers or were versed in the oral traditions. They shared both traditional stories and personal life-experience stories about ways to become a storyteller, cultural ways to use stories with children and adults, and ways to help people think, feel, and "be" through the power of stories.

The Elders taught me about seven principles related to using First Nations stories and storytelling for educational purposes, what I term storywork: respect, responsibility, reciprocity, reverence, holism, interrelatedness, and synergy. Experiential stories reinforce the need for storywork principles in order for one to use First Nations stories effectively. These seven principles form a Stó:lō and Coast Salish theoretical framework for making meaning from stories and for using them in educational contexts. I learned that stories can "take on their own life" and "become the teacher" if these principles are used.

During the journey Coyote and I learned that these storywork principles are like strands of a cedar basket. They have distinct shape in themselves, but when they are combined to create story meaning, they are transformed into new designs and also create the background, which shows the beauty of the designs. My learning and the stories contained in this book form a "storybasket" for others to use. Following Stó:lō tradition, I give back what I have learned about storywork, which effectively educates the heart, mind, body, and spirit.

The first chapter introduces Coyote the Trickster and the markers, or storywork principles, that guide travellers. The Indigenous storytellers who guided me to understandings of storywork through their written works are also introduced. A story told by Terry Tafoya entitled "Coyote's Eyes" is shared, and it continues to surface throughout the book at critical points.

Chapter 2 highlights my story research methodology with Elders. Respectful research relationships are portrayed through my experiences with three Elders: Chief Khot-La-Cha, Dr. Simon Baker; Tsimilano, Dr. Vincent Stogan; and Kwulasulwut, Dr. Ellen White. Showing respect through cultural protocol, appreciating the significance of and reverence for spirituality, honouring teacher and learner responsibilities, and practising a cyclical type of reciprocity are important lessons documented here for those interested in First Nations/Indigenous methodology.

Chapter 3 presents the teachings of the Stó:lō (Coqualeetza) Elders. I return "home" to talk with Elders in order to learn more about traditional aspects of becoming a storyteller and about cultural contexts for storytelling, and together we identify issues and educational possibilities for storywork. The Elders teach me about engaging in story research as methodology. They tell me enough to keep me curious, to keep me coming back to them for more teachings, and then they let me know that I must go away and make meaning from their talks.

In Chapter 4 I share my story of learning to become a storyteller and learning to appreciate the beauty and power embedded in stories. It is as though the story "comes alive" and becomes the teacher. I learn to use storywork first with Indigenous adult learners enrolled in a university program. The principles of holism, interrelatedness, and synergy work together to create powerful storywork understandings that have the power to help with emotional healing and wellness.

Chapter 5 shows the development of storywork through an elementary school curriculum project, First Nations Journeys of Justice. Working with community storytellers in respectful and responsible ways are highlighted, as are examples of culturally appropriate pedagogy.

Chapter 6 serves as a story summary of the seven theoretical storywork principles of respect, responsibility, reverence, reciprocity, holism, interrelatedness, and synergy. Implications for education, especially curricula and pedagogy, are discussed through teachers' experiences.

Chapter 7 has Coyote coming back in one last story with reminders of how culture can heal. Returning to the teachings of the Elders helped me to present – "share back" – and "give away" my learning through the metaphor of a storybasket. Persistent issues about story ownership, ethical use of stories, and how to keep the power of stories alive are discussed. Indigenous storywork is not easy, but it is essential if First Nations stories are to be used to educate the heart, mind, body, and spirit, which is truly Indigenous education.

In the book I use terms such as "First Nations," "Aboriginal," "Indigenous," and "Indian" interchangeably, as appropriate. If a particular term was preferred in a specific period or by a particular group, it is used. All terms are meant to include all people of Aboriginal ancestry.

ACKNOWLEDGMENTS

In Stó:lō tradition, I raise my hands in thanks and respect to the Elders with whom I learned, the Coqualeetza Elders, Drs. Simon Baker, Ellen White, and Vincent Stogan. The Elders' teachings kept me on the pathway to finding the cultural core of our stories, and they helped me to understand Indigenous storywork, despite some Coyote wanderings. Their Indigenous ways of teaching kept me coming back for more. Their teachings are embedded in my heart, mind, body, and spirit.

I raise my hands in thanks and respect to the following people who provided guidance and invaluable help during my research and writing journey: Celia Haig-Brown, Jean Barman, Carl Urion, Kieran Egan, Suzanne de Castell, Thomas Alcoze, Floy Pepper, and Sheila TeHenneppe. Thanks to John Claxton, my partner, who shared special conversations with me about this work.

The Stó:lō Nation education department's funding allowed me time to learn and engage in the story-research process – many thanks to Leslie Williams for his continual support. Additional publication funding from the BC Aboriginal Capacity and Development Research Environment (ACADRE) network, which came at a key moment, is greatly appreciated. Thanks to UBC Press, especially Jean Wilson, Robert Lewis, and Darcy Cullen for superb editorial assistance and for moving the manuscript along.

I raise my hands in thanks and respect to my family for their love and caring, to the family of the First Nations House of Learning, and to the Native Indian Teacher Education Program (NITEP) for encouragement, feedback, and nourishment when I needed it. Ongoing support and help from the Coqualeetza Cultural Centre staff, particularly Shirley Leon and Peter Lindley, made my return "home" very special. The staff of the Law Courts Education Society provided me with so many rich opportunities to engage with storytellers and storywork ideas, for which I am extremely grateful. I want to convey a special thanks to Corry, my daughter, who inspired me to do storywork as a way to improve Indigenous education for the younger and future generations.

Indigenous Storywork

CHAPTER ONE

The Journey Begins

Early this morning I asked for guidance from the Creator. The spiritual practice of prayer begins my day and my work. I have learned from First Nations Elders that beginning with a humble prayer creates a cultural learning process, which promotes the teachings of respect, reverence, responsibility, and reciprocity. I use the term "teachings" to mean cultural values, beliefs, lessons, and understandings that are passed from generation to generation. I am also thankful to Verna J. Kirkness and Ray Barnhardt (1991) for pointing out the importance of the "four R's" for Indigenous postsecondary education in their milestone article "First Nations and higher education: The four R's – respect, relevance, reciprocity, responsibility."

The particular Indigenous teachings that I use are both principles and practices that are interwoven throughout the book. Their application to Indigenous stories and storytelling recurs in each chapter, taking on additional meaning with each use. Understanding these cultural teachings and their application to learning will be an iterative process similar to that found in Chickasaw scholar Eber Hampton's "Towards a redefinition of Indian education." His thought and work "progresses in a spiral that adds a little with each thematic repetition rather than building an Aristotelian argument step-by-step ... I found new meaning in each turn of the spiral" (1995, 6). Eber Hampton uses a six-direction pattern: heaven, earth, north, south, east, and west. My cultural understandings are formed through learning relationships with Elders and challenged by experiential story wanderings with Coyote the Trickster.

I learn to weave the design of a Stó:lō and Coast Salish storytelling basket based on the storywork teachings of respect, reverence, responsibility, reciprocity, holism, interrelatedness, and synergy. Stó:lō women are known for their cedar baskets. Basket makers are often identified by their designs. In this book I use the basket as one metaphor for learning about stories and storytelling. Even though the design may be attributed to a particular person, her designs reflect her relationships with family, community, nation, land, and nature.

Sharing what one has learned is an important Indigenous tradition. This type of sharing can take the form of a story of personal life experience and is done with a compassionate mind and love for others. Walter Lightning (1992), of the Samson Cree Nation, learned that the compassionate mind combines physical, spiritual, emotional, and intellectual learning with humility, truth, and love.

A few years ago I had a dream and felt this kind of love and compassion from Stó:lō Elders.

MY DREAM

I was alone in a canoe and approaching land. There was a longhouse close to the water. As the canoe reached shore, many of the Old People came out to greet me. The Old Ones were those who had "passed on," or as we say, travelled to the Spirit World. I recognized many – Ed Leon, Teresa Michel, Susan Peters, Francis Kelly, Jean Silver – and some I did not know. As I walked closer to them, I started to cry. I cried because I realized at that moment how much I missed them. I told them that it was so hard living in the city and working at the university – living and working in a place where it was a constant struggle to be First Nations, to think and feel in a cultural way, and to be understood by others, the outsiders. I told them that I wanted to leave that cold place and stay with them. They put a woven blanket around me, like the one a Spokesperson wears in our cultural gatherings, and brought me into the longhouse. Inside, each one started talking to me.

All I could see was each one talking; it was like watching
a scene on television, but with the volume turned off. In
the dream, I could not hear what they were telling me. But
the talk went on for a long, long time. When it was finished,
they brought me outside and put me back in the canoe.
They said I had to go back, that I wouldn't be lonely anymore, and that I had important work to do yet.

For quite a while I pondered the meaning of this dream. It occurred
when I was beginning to do research about the oral tradition. I thought
that the dream was directing me to go on a "journey of learning," to
meet and learn from those who use the oral traditions, especially Elders.
I also felt that I needed to learn how to hear what the Elders had told
me in the dream. After learning how to listen to the stories, I was ex-
pected to use their cultural knowledge and to share it with others, thereby
ensuring its continuation. I have come to appreciate that dreams can be
a source of Indigenous knowledge and that they can provide guidance
for Indigenous research methodology (Castellano 2000; Marsden 2004;
Smith 1999).

Some teachings from my nation, the Stó:lō, are about cultural respect,
responsibility, and reciprocity. According to these teachings, important
knowledge and wisdom contain power. If one comes to understand and
appreciate the power of a particular knowledge, then one must be ready
to share and teach it respectfully and responsibly to others in order for
this knowledge, and its power, to continue. One cannot be said to have
wisdom until others acknowledge an individual's respectful and responsible use and teaching of knowledge to others. Usually, wisdom is attributed only to Elders, but this is not because they have lived a long
time. What one does with knowledge and the insight gained from knowledge are the criteria for being called an "Elder." Continuation of the
Stó:lō knowledge and power relationship happens through a reciprocal
process between teachers and learners.

My personal experiences of learning about the nature of Indigenous
stories, especially those of the Stó:lō and Coast Salish, and about their
application to education – storywork – are what I have to give back. I
coined the term "storywork" because I needed a term that signified that
our stories and storytelling were to be taken seriously. At Stó:lō cultural
gatherings, the Spokesman lets the guests know that it is time to pay

attention to the activities by saying, "My dear ones, our work is about to begin." Usually, the cultural work is witnessed by the guests through the oral tradition, which includes speech, story, and song.

To provide some further context for understanding how I came to appreciate the concept of storywork, I will share some personal background that brought me to the dream with the Elders. At our gatherings, speakers will identify their kinship and speak from their experiences. The Stó:lō geographical area encompasses the Fraser Valley of British Columbia. The estimated Stó:lō population is 5,700 (Carlson 1997). The Halq'emeylem[1] word "Stó:lō" means river. We are the River People. My relationship to the river, the land, and its resources has significantly influenced my identity. I grew up on the Soowahlie Reserve, near Cultus Lake. I am from the Kelly family. "Soowahlie" means "to dissolve or disappear." My mother is from the Diablo/James family of the St'at'imc Nation, Xaxl'ip Fountain Reserve, Lillooet, British Columbia. The languages and cultures of the Stó:lō and St'at'imc are different.[2]

From 1976 to 1983 I worked in my home area, the Stó:lō Nation, with the Coqualeetza Cultural Centre, the Coqualeetza Elders, and the Stó:lō Sitel curriculum project. I was employed as an elementary school teacher with the Chilliwack School District and as the curriculum consultant for Coqualeetza. The centre's Halq'emeylem name, "Coqualeetza," is the word for a gathering and cleansing place where people met, in traditional times, to wash their blankets. The Coqualeetza Elders and the Coqualeetza staff were instrumental in planning, developing, and implementing an elementary-level social studies curriculum called the Stó:lō Sitel. "Sitel" is the word for a basket used to store treasures.

An important aspect of the curriculum in which I was involved focused on First Nations cultural stories. During the seven-year period of this work, I was fortunate to hear many traditional and life-experience stories told at Elders' meetings, at cultural gatherings like the summer fish camp, funerals, and feasts, and in personal conversation. These stories created good memories of feeling loved by the Elders and started an appreciation of the intellectual, emotional, spiritual, and physical teachings that were embedded in the stories. Some of these beginning teachings were introduced in the Stó:lō Sitel lessons.

I left the Stó:lō area in 1985 and moved to Vancouver to work at the University of British Columbia (UBC) with the Native Indian Teacher Education Program. In 1989 I enrolled in a PhD program at Simon Fraser University, which I completed while continuing to teach at UBC. I also served as the director of the First Nations House of Learning at UBC, and I am currently the associate dean for Indigenous education in the Faculty of Education.

One educational goal that I had for my doctoral work was to find a way to fully examine Indigenous knowledges and Indigenous ways of knowing within academe. I also wanted to demonstrate that Indigenous knowledge systems could be investigated from an Indigenous perspective with rigour acceptable to the academy. Along the way, I decided to focus on the topic of Indigenous stories, even though at the time I did not have a full appreciation of their power. The experience of working with the Elders and the Stó:lō Sitel curriculum project greatly influenced my choice. Along the way I found Coyote.

Finding Coyote

On my research journey I met many gifted and caring storytellers who readily shared their stories and understandings of the oral traditions. Many with whom I talked became new friends. With my "old" friends, a new dynamic to our friendship emerged as we shared story experiences. One of the new friends was Coyote. Among many First Nations, Coyote and her/his/its many manifestations is considered a Trickster character who has lots to learn and teach while travelling the world. The English word "trickster" is a poor one because it cannot portray the diverse range of ideas that First Nations associate with the Trickster, who sometimes is like a magician, an enchanter, an absurd prankster, or a Shaman, who sometimes is a shape shifter, and who often takes on human characteristics. Trickster is a transformer figure, one whose transformations often use humour, satire, self-mocking, and absurdity to carry good lessons. Other well-known Trickster characters include Raven, Wesakejac, Nanabozo, and Glooscap. Trickster often gets into trouble by ignoring cultural rules and practices or by giving sway to the negative aspects of "humanness," such as vanity, greed, selfishness, and foolishness. Trickster seems to learn lessons the hard way and sometimes not at all. At the same time, Trickster has the ability to do good things for others and is sometimes like a powerful spiritual being and given much respect.

Trickster characters like Coyote have existed in our stories since "time immemorial," as our people say. Each First Nations culture has particular attributes and types of teachings connected to the Trickster. Often tribal Tricksters nearly die, or they die and then are resurrected. Perhaps one of the most important characteristics of the tribal Trickster related to my storytelling research is Gerald Vizenor's notion that she/he/it needs communal and land connections:

> The trickster is in a comic world, surviving by his wits, prevailing in good humor. He's in a collective, hardly ever in isolation. When he is in isolation, he's almost always in trouble, in a life-threatening situation he has to get out of through ritual or symbolic acts. Through reversals he has to get back to connections to imagination, to people, to places. (1987, 295)

Vizenor, who is of the Minnesota Chippewa Nation, believes that the Trickster is a "doing, not an essence, not a museum being, not an aesthetic presence" (13).

The notion of the Trickster as a "doing" rather than a "being" fits with how I have come to appreciate the process of learning through Trickster stories. The Trickster as a doing can change and live on through time as people interact with the Trickster through stories; one does not have to be too concerned about what the Trickster looks like if she/he/it is a doing rather than a being. This notion of the tribal Trickster lets me interact with her/him/it. Coyote, then, helps me to reflect and to gain understandings, challenging and comforting me just like a critical friend.

Contemporary Aboriginal storytellers and writers relate to the characteristics and roles of the tribal Trickster in various ways. Sherman Alexie, of the Spokane/Coeur d'Alene people of Washington, uses analogies to define a Coyote Trickster that intersect with North American popular culture:

From Thomas Builds-the-Fire's Journal:

Coyote: A small canid (Canis latrans) native to western North America that is closely related to the American wolf and whose cry has often been compared to that of Sippie Wallace and Janis Joplin, among others.

Coyote: A traditional figure in Native American mythology, alternately responsible for the creation of the earth and for some of the more ignorant acts after the fact.

Coyote: A trickster whose bag of tricks contains permutations of love, hate, weather, chance, laughter, and tears, e.g. Lucille Ball. (1995, 48)

Tomson Highway, of the Cree Nation, said that without the Trickster, "the core of Indian culture would be gone forever" (quoted in Acoose 1993, 37). He notes that the role of the Trickster "is to teach us about the nature and the meaning of existence on the planet Earth" (38). Lenore Keeshig-Tobias, a Chippewas of the Nawash First Nation (also called Cape Croker), points out the paradoxical role of the Trickster as teacher: "Christ-like in a way. Except that from our Teacher, we learn through the Teacher's mistakes as well as the [T]eacher's virtues" (quoted in Acoose 1993, 38).

Coyote stories and other Indigenous stories appear here sometimes upon invitation, sometimes unexpectedly. How Coyote sees the world and comes to make sense of it through interrelationships is critical to understanding the lessons that I learned about Indigenous storywork and researching with Elders.

When I began to delve into the topic of Indigenous stories, the first contradiction that I faced was that I had to complete academic work steeped in literacy, analysis, and explicitness. However, the topic of Indigenous stories, which were presumably based on oral delivery and aural reception and were sometimes thought to have implicit meanings, conflicted with the academic literate traditions. Indigenous stories have lost much educational and social value due to colonization, which resulted in weak translations from Aboriginal languages to English, stories shaped to fit a Western literate form, and stories adapted to fit a predominantly Western education system. The translations lose much of the original humour and meaning and are misinterpreted and/or appropriated by those who don't understand the story connections and cultural teachings. I did not want to perpetuate this loss. Instead, I wanted to find a way to respectfully place First Nations stories within the academic and educational mileux.

The story "Coyote's Eyes," told and written by Terry Tafoya[3] (1982), spoke to me about oral-literate contradictions, which can be viewed in various ways. This story was put into a written version for an educational journal. Tafoya's way of bringing together the oral tradition and academe created a pathway for me to follow.

Leslie Marmon Silko, of the Laguna Pueblo Nation, New Mexico, provides us with an important signpost for story listening that can be applied to the stories presented in this book:

For those of you accustomed to being taken from point A to point B to point C, this presentation may be somewhat difficult to follow. Pueblo expression resembles something like a spider's web – with many little threads radiating from the centre, crisscrossing one another. As with the web, the structure emerges as it is made, and you must simply listen and trust, as the Pueblo people do, that meaning will be made. (1996, 48-49)

Patience and trust are essential for preparing to listen to stories. Listening involves more than just using the auditory sense. We must visualize the characters and their actions. We must let our emotions surface. As the Elders say, it is important to listen with "three ears: two on the sides of our head and the one that is in our heart."

COYOTE'S EYES

Long time ago, when mountains were the size of salmon eggs, Coyote was going along, and saw that Rabbit was doing something. Now, this Rabbit was a Twati, an Indian doctor, and as Coyote watched, Rabbit sang his spirit song, and the Rabbit's eyes flew out of his head and perched on a tree branch. Rabbit called out, "Whee-num, come here," and his eyes returned to their empty sockets.

This greatly impressed Coyote, who immediately begged Rabbit to teach him how to do this.

Rabbit said no.

Coyote begged.

Rabbit said no.

"Oh, please," cried Coyote.

"No," replied Rabbit.

"But it's such a wonderful trick! Teach me."

"No."

"But I'll do exactly as you say!"

"I will teach you," said Rabbit, "but you must never do this more than four times in one day, or something terrible will happen to you." And so Rabbit taught Coyote his spirit song, and soon Coyote's eyes flew up and perched on a tree.

"Whee-num! Come here!" called Coyote, and his eyes returned to him.

Now Rabbit left, and Coyote kept practicing. He sent his eyes back and forth to the tree four times. Then he thought, "I should show off this new trick to the Human People, instead of just doing it for myself."

So Coyote went to the nearest Indian village, and yelled out for all the people to gather around him. With his new audience, Coyote sang the Rabbit's song, and the crowd was very impressed to see his eyes fly out of his head and perch on the branch of a tree.

"Whee-num!" Coyote called out. His eyes just sat on the tree and looked down at him. The Indian people started to laugh.

"Come here!" shouted Coyote. His eyes just looked at him.

"Whee-num!" Just then a crow flew by, and spotting the eyes, thought they were berries. The crow swooped down and ate them.

Now Coyote was blind, and staggered out of the village, hoping to find new eyes. He heard the sounds of running water, and felt around, trying to find the stream. Now, around flowing water, one finds bubbles, and Coyote tried to take these bubbles and use them for eyes. But bubbles soon pop, and that's what Coyote discovered.

Now Coyote felt around and discovered huckleberries, so he took those and used them for eyes. But huckleberries are so dark, everything looked black. Now Coyote was really feeling sorry for himself.

"Eenee snawai, I'm just pitiful," Coyote cried.

"Why are you so sad?" asked a small voice, for little mouse had heard him.

"My dear Cousin," said Coyote, "I've lost my eyes ... I'm blind, and I don't know what to do."

"Snawai Yunwai," replied Mouse. "You poor thing. I have two eyes, so I will share one with you." Having said this, Mouse removed one of his eyes and handed it to Coyote. Now Coyotes are much larger than mice, and when Coyote dropped Mouse's eye into his socket, it just rolled around in the big empty space. The new eye was so small it only let in a tiny amount of light. It was like looking at the world through a little hole.

Coyote walked on, still feeling sorry for himself, just barely able to get around with Mouse's eye. "Eenee snawai, I'm just pitiful," he sobbed.

"Why are you crying, Coyote?" asked Buffalo in his deep voice.

"Oh Cousin," began Coyote, "all I have to see with is this tiny eye of Mouse. It's so small it only lets in a little bit of light, so I can barely see."

"Snawai Yunwai," replied Buffalo. "You poor thing, I have two eyes, so I will share one with you." Then Buffalo took out one of his eyes and handed it to Coyote. Now Buffaloes are much larger than Coyotes, and when Coyote tried to squeeze Buffalo's eye into his other socket, it hung over into the rest of his face. So large was Buffalo's eye that it let in so much light, Coyote was nearly blinded by the glare ... everything looked twice as large as it ordinarily did. And so, Coyote was forced to continue his journey, staggering about with his mismatched eyes. (Tafoya 1982, 21-22)

Terry Tafoya shares one of many meanings from this story. He says, "Coyote, in his normal state represents a bit of everything. He must not be understood by knowing only one legend, but in the context of the many legends in which he and his counterparts in other tribes appear" (1982, 22). Throughout this book other Coyote stories and other Indigenous stories and views about oral tradition are shared to build the kind of holistic context that Tafoya implies. Over the years this story has become important to my teaching and learning, as other meanings unfold in various contexts.

At the end of the story, Coyote staggers because he has only "accommodated the elements of Mouse and Buffalo into his strategies; he is not very successful because he has not learned balance. To be a whole human being (one might say a complete Coyote), one must learn to switch back and forth between the eyes of not only Mouse and Buffalo, but ... all the other animals of legend" (Tafoya 1982, 24).

The other animals have cultural symbolic meanings too, and their relationships with Coyote must be understood. Thomas King, who is of Cherokee descent, describes the positive effect of Trickster's learning in bringing about balance: "The trickster is an important figure ... it allows us to create a particular kind of world in which the Judeo-Christian concern with good and evil and order and disorder is replaced with the more Native concern for balance and harmony" (1990, xiii). The balance and harmony discussed by Tafoya and King depend on understanding the concept of First Nations holism, sometimes symbolized by the medicine wheel (Battiste 2000; Bopp et al. 1984; Cajete 1994; Calliou

1995; Graveline 1998; Pepper and Henry 1991) and sometimes by the sacred circle of life (Sioui 1992).

Holism: Creating a Context for Orality

An Indigenous philosophical concept of holism refers to the interrelatedness between the intellectual, spiritual (metaphysical values and beliefs and the Creator), emotional, and physical (body and behaviour/action) realms to form a whole healthy person. The development of holism extends to and is mutually influenced by one's family, community, band, and nation. The image of a circle is used by many First Nations peoples to symbolize wholeness, completeness, and ultimately wellness. The never-ending circle also forms concentric circles to show both the synergistic influence of and our responsibility toward the generations of ancestors, the generations of today, and the generations yet to come. The animal/human kingdoms, the elements of nature/land, and the Spirit World are an integral part of the concentric circles (see Figure 1).[4]

Each Indigenous group has developed its own cultural content for the holistic circle symbol; however, a common goal has been to attain a mutual balance and harmony among animals, people, elements of nature, and the Spirit World. To attain this goal, ways of acquiring knowledge and codes of behaviour are essential and are embedded in cultural practices; one practice that plays a key role in the oral tradition is storytelling. Some stories remind us about being whole and healthy

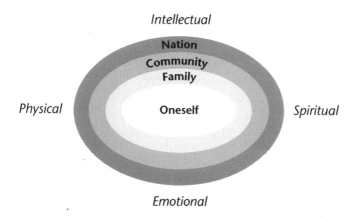

Figure 1   Holism: A context for Indigenous storywork

and remind us of traditional teachings that have relevance to our lives. Stories have the power to make our hearts, minds, bodies, and spirits work together. When we lose a part of ourselves, we lose balance and harmony, and we may feel like Coyote with the mismatched eyes. Only when our hearts, minds, bodies, and spirits work together do we truly have Indigenous education.

Coyote's situation could also be a metaphor to show the relationship between orality (oral traditions) and literacy, or it could be about the relationship between Indigenous storytellers and academic researchers. At first, I likened the small eye to our oral tradition, which has been denigrated and diminished through Western literate influences. The large eye representing the Western literate traditions has often assumed an overpowering position, especially in educational contexts. Other times, the small eye became the research method, and the large eye represented Indigenous theory. Coyote was given the challenge of making her/his/its eyes work together, in harmony and balance, in order to have a clearer view of the world. I was challenged to bring together, in harmony and balance, a First Nations knowledge and way of knowing and research methodology. In this book I show how Elders helped me to understand an important dimension of First Nations/Indigenous knowledge through stories.

On this journey I asked those who travelled on story pathways about the nature of stories, how they were traditionally used for teaching and learning purposes, and how to mindfully place Indigenous stories in education today. I use Gregory Cajete's (1994) Navajo definition of pathways: "path" symbolizes a journey and a process; "way" is a cultural, philosophical framework. I have been taught that Elders who have "tried to live their life right, just like a story," to borrow the phrase from Yukon First Nations Elder Mrs. Smith (quoted in Cruikshank et al. 1990, 1), are respected teachers because they have tried to be "good" human beings by seeking guidance in the traditional teachings at the core of Indigenous stories. Gregory Cajete, a Tewa Indian of the Santa Clara Pueblo, New Mexico, provides a definition of this kind of goodness:

> The Indigenous ideal of living "a good life" in Indian traditions is at times referred to by Indian people as striving "to always think the highest thought" ... Thinking the highest thought means thinking of one's self, one's community, and one's environment richly. This thinking in the highest, most respectful, and compassionate way systematically

influences the actions of both individuals and the community. It is a way to perpetuate "a good life," a respectful and spiritual life, a wholesome life. (1994, 46)

Not all Elders are storytellers, and not all Elders have lived a good life. But to learn the highest degree of cultural knowledge, one could go to an Elder or someone not yet an Elder who understands and who lives the "good" cultural traditions. One could also go to someone who has good teachings. Walter Lightning describes the authority that Elders use to teach: "When [Elders] teach others they very often begin by quoting the authority of Elders who have gone before. They do not state the authority as coming from themselves. They will say things like 'This is what they used to say,' or 'This is what they said'" (1992, 242).

Following this teaching and type of authority, this book is about what Elders and others who tried to live their lives right, just like a story, told me. My challenge was to hear and remember what they said and to share or represent their teachings respectfully, responsibly, and accurately. Imagine that I am now the Coyote with the mismatched eyes, wandering around, wondering how I will get out of the predicament where the oral and literate worlds are in conflict. Instead of being self-absorbed in pity, I am lucky and encounter others who have travelled on the pathways of the oral traditions and who have shared their understandings through a literate medium that is shaped by the framework and message of the oral ways.

It is important to note that the oral tradition still lives, and the written tradition is growing within it, not exempt from it. The one will never replace the other. The elements of old stories, of the spoken language, the myths and narratives that sustain the culture, and the speech patterns of the elders occur over and over again in the new writing. (Dauenhauer, Dauenhauer, and Holthaus 1986, 10-11)

Coming to Terms with Oral and Written Ways

Losing the "eyes," or the understanding, of a worldview embedded in Aboriginal oral traditions, particularly in the stories, is strongly linked to the legacy of forced colonization and assimilation during the missionary and residential-school eras and then through the public schooling system (Archibald 1993; Ashworth 1979; Battiste 2000; Haig-Brown 1988; Kirkness 1981; Royal Commission on Aboriginal Peoples 1996b).

An Indigenous life-experience story recounted by anthropologist Barre Toelken exemplifies the detrimental influence of schooling and academic literacy on the ability to make story meaning in a traditional way and illustrates how this affects the storytelling relationship between a Navajo Elder, Little Wagon, and the Elder's grandson. The grandson asks Little Wagon where snow comes from. In response, the grandfather tells a story about an ancestor who found some beautiful burning material, which he kept burning until the owners, the Spirits, asked for it. The Spirits wanted to reward the finder, but because the material was so precious, they asked him to complete very difficult feats to test his patience and endurance. After he successfully completed them, the Spirits told him that in return for his fine behaviour they would throw all the ashes from their own fireplace down into Montezuma Canyon each year when they cleaned house. Little Wagon closes the story: "Sometimes they fail to keep their word; but in all, they turn their attention toward us regularly, here in Montezuma Canyon" (Toelken and Scott 1981, 73). After awhile the grandson asks why it snows in another area. The Elder tells the boy that he will have to make his own story to answer that question. Much later, Little Wagon told Toelken that it was too bad his grandson did not understand stories. Toelken explains the lesson/point that he learned:

> I found by questioning him that he did not in fact consider it an etiological story and did not in any way believe that that was the way snow originated; rather, if the story was about anything it was about moral values, about the deportment of a young protagonist whose actions showed a properly reciprocal relationship between himself and nature. In short, by seeing the story in terms of any categories I had been taught to recognize, I had missed the point; and so had our young visitor, a fact which Little Wagon at once attributed to the deadly influences of white schooling. (73)

Little Wagon was right about the "deadly influence of white schooling," which contributed to the diminishing influence of the oral tradition when institutionalized schooling and its essayist form of literacy (Scollon and Scollon 1981) were forced upon First Nations. Colonized assimilation and acculturation predominantly through education forced Western literacy, values, and ways of thinking upon generations of Aboriginal people. Aboriginal languages, and hence our forms of orality (oral tradition in practice), were prohibited in the residential schools.

More life-experience stories about children being harshly punished for speaking their language and about the intergenerational trauma of residential-school abuse are being told and published (Chrisjohn, Young, and Maraun 1997; Haig-Brown 1988; Ing 2000; Jaine 1993; Knockwood 1992; Milloy 1999; Royal Commission on Aboriginal Peoples 1996b; Sterling 1992). Public schooling continued the colonial assault on Aboriginal children (Archibald 1995; Battiste 2000). Western-oriented educational institutions displaced Aboriginal cultural worldviews and our oral traditions with various forms of literacy.

The story about Coyote's eyes made me examine the shifting relationship between Indigenous orality and Western literacy. At first, I positioned orality and literacy in a dichotomous relationship because their principles and characteristics seemed so different and conflictual. Perhaps I did this because historically First Nations and anything considered "Western" have usually been described as being different from each other and in opposition. The benefit of clearly separating the two was that I began to explore a pathway that led me to understand the strength of Indigenous orality. For four years I learned from Elders and other storytellers about the characteristics of the oral tradition and stories.

I also examined the topic of orality and its relationship to literacy through the lens of various respected Western scholars, such as Eric Havelock (1963, 1986), Walter Ong (1971, 1982), Jack Goody (1977), David Olson (1987), and Kieran Egan (1987, 1988). Their understandings of oral cultures are derived either from examinations of Greek orality or from the work of other non-Indigenous academics who studied and wrote about Indigenous oral cultures.[5] I appreciated their perspectives and valued the academic space that they opened for me to examine Indigenous orality. However, after many attempts to fit these perspectives into my research, I finally realized that in formulating their paradigms I was making the same mistake as Toelken had when viewing Little Wagon's story with categories that did not fit – hence my lack of success. Initially, I presented "evidence" that First Nations orality had "good" forms of thinking (Egan 1987) and that it had some of Ong's components of his "psychodynamics of orality" (1982, 28-37). I did this exercise because I felt that it was important to counter the notion that the knowledge contained in the oral traditions of Aboriginal people is not as intellectually challenging as that found in Western forms of literacy – the literacy hypothesis put forth by Goody (1977), Olson (1987), and Ong (1982).

By engaging in this type of comparison, however, I was missing the point of learning from Indigenous oral tradition and from those who know about it and have shared it with others in a literate form. I was also caught in a theorizing dilemma. Kimberly Blaeser from the White Earth Reservation in Minnesota, who is of Ojibway ancestry, has identified Western theoretical models as inappropriate for application to American Indian literature/stories: "The insistence on reading Native literature by way of Western literary theory clearly violates its integrity and performs a new act of colonization and conquest" (1993, 55). In this newer context "colonization" means "authority emanating from the mainstream critical center to the marginalized native texts" (56). Even though Blaeser refers only to literary theory, literacy can have the same colonizing influence on our literature – our stories. To get away from this "new act of colonization," I had to read and hear the voices of First Nations/Indigenous peoples and find the theories embedded in their stories. Kimberly Blaeser echoes these reminders: "We must first 'know the stories of our people' and then 'make our own story too' ... we must 'be aware of the way they [Western literary theorists] change the stories we already know' for only with that awareness can we protect the integrity of the Native American story" (61).

To provide an understanding of Indigenous perspectives about storytelling, I use works written by Elders and other Indigenous storytellers whom I consider to be the first wave of Indigenous scholars to start an Indigenous corpus of literature about storytelling.[6] At Stó:lō cultural gatherings we give the "floor" to respected speakers whom we ask to speak. A carved talking stick, held by the designated speaker, is an example of a cultural protocol reinforcing that this speaker has been given time to share her or his knowledge through the oral tradition – whether as story, speech, or song. Once the speaker is finished, the talking stick may be given to the next speaker. Sometimes, speakers will have their own talking sticks with carved designs that have particular meaning related to their family or community histories. This book speaks about or shows how Indigenous storytellers and scholars effectively use written text to discuss Elders' story-related teachings, shows characteristics of stories, and discusses the power of storytelling for teaching and learning purposes. Through the knowledge and experiences embedded in the first-wave literature, we can find principles that address the politics of accessing publishers and producing publications, the authority to tell stories, and the need to establish collaborative relationships between First Nations Elders and storytellers and non-First Nations educators.

Writing about Oral Tradition: Indigenous Perspectives

> Indian elders often remind young people to live the myths by saying,
> "These stories, this language, these ways, and this land are the only
> valuables we can give you – but life is in them for those who know
> how to ask and how to learn." (Cajete 1994, 41)

My concern about the negative influence of literacy faded to the background as I found more books and articles related to the oral tradition that were written by Indigenous people.[7] As I examined what they had to say about stories and storytelling, I noted how these storytellers used text to portray their oral tradition. Sometimes Indigenous perspectives are presented without explicit comment – in accordance with the oral tradition of letting the listener, now reader, make meaning from someone's words and stories without direction from the storyteller. Whenever Indigenous oral tradition is presented in textual form, the text limits the level of understanding because it cannot portray the storyteller's gestures, tone, rhythm, and personality.

The journal *BC Studies* dedicated an issue entitled *In celebration of our survival* exclusively to First Nations peoples, their voices, and their ways of sharing their knowledges. The editors, Doreen Jensen and Cheryl Brooks, both Aboriginal women, wanted to acknowledge and celebrate Aboriginal peoples' ability to survive decades of colonization and forced assimilation and asked knowledgeable Aboriginal people who were also well-known orators to contribute articles. Jensen and Brooks articulate a respectful approach that arose as a reaction against a commonly experienced disrespectful one:

> As we planned for this publication, we debated how we should limit
> and focus the content, but ultimately decided that perhaps that has
> been part of the problem in the past: Native people have always been
> asked for their comments on and contributions to established agenda
> topics rather than simply being requested to tell their own story. So our
> contributors were invited to write about what they personally felt was
> important in painting a portrait of our people. (1991, 10)

The Aboriginal people who contributed to this journal issue used stories of personal experience, poetry, art, "talks" about traditional teachings, and critical essays about historical, political, and cultural issues to present various and diverse portraits of Aboriginal life.

Jeannette Armstrong, of the Okanagan Nation, also edited a collection of Native academic essays about First Nations literature and First Nations literary analysis, *Looking at the words of our people: First Nations analysis of literature.* In her words: "I felt that gathering a collection of Native academic voices on First Nations Literature is one way I can insist on listening to First Nations analysis and the best way to contribute to the dialogue on English Literature and First Nations Voice within literature itself" (1993, 8). Armstrong insists that "the questioning must first be an acknowledgment and recognition that the voices are culture-specific voices and that there are experts within those cultures who are essential to be drawn from and drawn out in order to incorporate into the reinterpretation through pedagogy, the context of English Literature coming from Native Americans" (7).

It is through these types of written forums that First Nations discourses – ways of thinking, talking, and representing our knowledges and perspectives in a scholarly context – become evident. Carl Urion, who is of Dearborn River Métis ancestry, notes two critical considerations about First Nations discourse that he has observed: (1) "it assumes a context in which there is unity and wholeness to be discovered or reaffirmed"; and (2) "the relationship between a person of moral authority and another person creates the discourse; it is created anew in each generation; it changes, but maintains its stability and its internal organization" (1991, 5). I now believe that one who has tried to live her/his life "right" by practising the values of respect, reverence, responsibility, and reciprocity is one who may have the kind of moral authority referred to by Urion. His considerations are process-oriented, and he notes that the meanings derived through First Nations discourse require constant thinking about and playing with "levels of metaphor and implication" (5). Linda Akan, of the Saulteaux Nation, also writes about First Nations thought using what may seem like a playful metaphor, but this metaphor has insight for those who understand its implications:

If one were to try to give a metaphorical description of some of the features of First Nations thought, one might say that [in order to acquire these thoughts one would] go to school in dreams, write in iconographic imagery, travel in Trickster's vehicle, talk in metaphor, and always walk around. (1992, 213)

The issues and the way that we want to deal with the issues – the types of conversations and talks – must be given space for us to fill. This does not mean that non-Native people should be forever excluded from the conversations, only that First Nations people need some space to talk so that we can share our stories in our own way and create discourses based on our Indigenous knowledge systems. Then we can open the conversation for others to join.

There is a lot of rhetoric about the "voices" of First Nations people being presented through written text. How does one assess the cultural content coming from the many voices, and who has authority to speak? Basil Johnston, an Ojibwa storyteller and author, provides an answer based on traditional reverence for speech and its strong connection to truth:

> Words are medicine that can heal or injure ... To instill respect for language the old counselled youth, "Don't talk too much," ... for they saw a kinship between language and truth. The expression is not without its facetious aspect but in its broader application it was intended to convey to youth other notions implicit in the expression "Don't talk too much," for the injunction also meant "Don't talk too often ... Don't talk too long ... Don't talk about those matters that you know nothing about." Were a person to restrict his discourse, and measure his speech, and govern his talk by what he knew, he would earn the trust and respect of his [or her] listeners ... people would want to hear the speaker again and by so doing bestow upon the speaker the opportunity to speak, for ultimately it is the people who confer the right of speech by their audience. (1990, 12)

Johnston shows a relationship between truth, respect, and trust that could serve as a criterion for determining the credibility of one's words. He goes on to describe the high regard given to those who skilfully and respectfully practised the oral tradition and introduces a negative effect of literacy, which separated the speaker from the listener:

> Language was a precious heritage; literature was no less precious. So precious did the tribe regard language and speech that it held those who abused language and speech and truth in contempt and ridicule and withheld them from their trust and confidence. To the tribe the man or woman who rambled on and on, who let his tongue range over every subject or warp the truth was said to talk in circles in a manner no different from that of a mongrel who, not knowing the source of alarm, barks in circles. Ever since words and sounds were reduced to written

symbols and have been stripped of their mystery and magic, the regard and reverence for them have diminished in tribal life. (12-13)

The mystery, magic, and truth/respect/trust relationship between the speaker/storyteller and listener/reader may be brought to life on the printed page if the principles of the oral tradition are used. A few Canadian Aboriginal people have persisted and managed to publish their traditional and life-experience stories using principles from their oral traditions: George Clutesi (1967, 1969, 1990), Ellen White (1981, 2006), Verna J. Kirkness (1994), Maria Campbell (1973, 1995), and Shirley Sterling (1997, 2002). There are Native American storytellers and writers who have been greatly influenced by the study of oral traditions, such as N. Scott Momaday (1969), Leslie Marmon Silko (1981), Paula Gun Allen (1986, 1989), Gerald Vizenor (1987), Greg Sarris (1993, 1994), Craig Womack (1999), and Thomas King (2003), whose work will be referred to in other parts of this book.

The late George Clutesi was among the first Aboriginal people in British Columbia to publish stories from his culture, that of the Tse-shaht people of Vancouver Island. Entitled *Fables of the Tse-shaht people: Son of Raven, son of Deer* (1967) and *Potlatch* (1969), both were used in the public school system. In 1969 George Clutesi spoke to a group of First Nations university students; I was one of them. He was an inspirational yet humble speaker. I felt very proud to identify with him as an Indian person. At the time, there were very few Aboriginal people who had published books that had been included in school curricula. Today, as I look at the book *Potlatch* and read the jacket cover, written by someone else, I am angered by the patronizing tone of the outsider's language. Today, such language would not be accepted, but colonial attitudes and approaches still persist.[8] However, the writer was right about George Clutesi leading white children to "deeper understanding":

In 1967, during Canada's Centennial Year, Mr. Clutesi was commissioned to paint a large mural at Expo and [published] his first book. *Son of Raven, Son of Deer* appeared and headed for immediate success. Now his message was coming through strong and clear. The final accolade after years of struggle was the selection of this first book as an elementary English text in British Columbia schools. Indian children making an appearance in schools outside the reserves are delighted to find a text written by one of their own race. White children discover in George Clutesi an Indian Aesop who leads them to deeper understanding.

In the foreword to *Potlatch,* George Clutesi tells us: "This narrative is not meant to be documentary. In fact it is meant to evade documents. It is meant for the reader to feel and to say I was there and indeed I saw." The power of the storyteller to make the listeners/readers visualize events and feel like they are part of the story is a principle that I have heard from others and that will be exemplified in later chapters. George Clutesi died before his last book, *Stand tall, my son,* was published. In this book he wrote about the education of a young boy, a member of a Northwest Coast culture, through stories, talks, and art; the themes of tradition, change, survival, and strength are strongly presented. Mr. Clutesi was a very respected orator, artist, and educator. His legacy of knowledge, wisdom, and philosophy has been left to those who take the time and effort to learn from his teachings.

> We, as a nation, possess many admirable qualities. We still have enough patience. We still listen before we utter. There are yet among us admirable teachers endowed with empathy and compassion. Seek for their knowledge especially during your quest and sojourn in the alien world of technology ... Among other qualities, your people as a whole possess a voice that soothes and calms the whole being. (1990, 169)

Verna J. Kirkness, of the Cree Nation of Manitoba and a well-known educator, compiled and edited the life story of Dr. Simon Baker, of the Squamish Nation: *Khot-La-Cha: The autobiography of Chief Simon Baker.* He asked Verna to help him present his life story through a book – and in his own way. His motive for publishing his life story, based on the principles of cultural responsibility and reciprocity, has been echoed by many Elders:

> I would like to tell about my life, what I've seen, what I've done, so my grandchildren and their children will learn things that happened in this last hundred years. I believe that my story will be interesting for schools. I know when I go to schools today, kindergartens or even high school, the children like to hear about my life. They enjoy my songs that my elders taught me many years ago. I sing to them in my language and often I tell them the story of my people, using my talking stick. (1994, xi)

Chief Khot-La-Cha continued his teaching responsibility by creating educational material that could be used in school curricula. His autobiography shows how life-experience stories can teach about culture, nature, history, politics, leadership, family relationships, and the importance of Elders. He stresses his people's teachings about relationships to nature's resources, the importance of spirituality, and the benefits of cultural knowledge:

> I was born and raised by the river. Water is very important. Our old people used to say, "water is your best friend." They would tell us to go and swim even when we were just toddlers. Mother Earth gave us water and we were taught ... It goes in a cycle. If we didn't have water we would perish ... water gives you a new life, a good feeling (Kirkness 1994, 155).

> We have gone too long in the wrong direction. We were a spiritual people. We paid great homage to our Creator and we must get back to that way of thinking. Spirituality, culture and [Native] language must be emphasized for our young people to know who they are. Education is the tool necessary for self-determination ... it will take time. First of all, our young people need pride. (176)

Simon Baker tape-recorded many of the political meetings and talks that he had with his *tillicums*/friends. Many years ago there was a concern among First Nations people about not recognizing the important contribution that Elders can make. One such historic meeting was held in 1976 to discuss the provincial disunity of British Columbia First Nations, and the role of the Elder "kept coming up" (181). Baker's thoughts on the matter echo those of the late George Clutesi, cited above:

> We must ask ourselves how we can best get back together ... We the old-timers, old men and old women, are feeling bad because we seem to have been thrown aside because our usefulness has been considered to be at an end. Friends, in the old Indian tradition, in the old Indian philosophy, in the old Indian teachings, the older you get, the more you will be needed. The sooner the young people realize this the sooner we can work together like one good family. (183)

Since that time, the role of Elders has gained prominence, especially in education. Today, there are First Nations Elders who have made and continue to make significant epistemological and social contributions at all levels of education. We are fortunate that Elders like Dr. Simon Baker have given inspiration, good teachings, and quality leadership to many. Unfortunately, many of these Elders are now passing on to the Spirit World.

> I'm in the last cycle. People are coming to ask me, "What did you do in the past? What can we do in the future to teach our children?" We are faced with so many things, violence, drugs, alcohol. So we're going back to our culture, to the old ways; taking our children back into the longhouse, taking them into the sweat lodge ... It's coming back strong. The cycle of healing. We're healing a lot of people of the suffering when they went to [residential] school ... Their cycle is coming back. They're giving themselves back to the Great Spirit. It is good to sit with an elder. It is good medicine for us. We like to talk. When the day is finished, I like to think I did something for today. Tomorrow is another day. (Kirkness 1994, 173)

David Neel, a photographer, artist, and writer of the Kwagiutl Nation, talked with forty-seven Northwest Coast Elders and leaders for his book *Our chiefs and elders: Words and photographs of Native leaders.* He combines photography and the talks, which have been edited very little, to present "a statement of the surviving race" (1992, 11). This work is in contrast to the much earlier approach of Edward Curtis, who promoted the "vanishing race" myth. Neel also acknowledges the critical need for Elders' teachings and shares important lessons that he learned about respect and responsibility during his work:

> Today, the role and knowledge of elders are being preserved and respected to the best ability of the people. The roles of elders vary from area to area and from family to family. Throughout the Coast area they are recognized as a great resource. Elders often play a role in the political process as well as in the general culture. It is their inherited knowledge, as well as their perspective (derived from experience), which is valued. In the Native way, memory or history is a tribal or family responsibility and is held and passed on by elders.
>
> ... Respect is the foundation for all relationships: between individuals, with future and past generations, with the Earth, with animals, with our Creator ... and with ourselves. To understand [respect] and apply it to our lives is an ongoing process. This is the most valuable

lesson the leaders have for us. It is not a lesson that can be explained
with the simple formula [or definition], "Respect is ..." (22)

Maria Campbell, a Métis author, filmmaker, teacher, activist, and storyteller, translated *Stories of the Road Allowance People,* as told by some of
the "old men." She describes the comfortable family-like context for
storytelling and how she was directed to learn from the old men rather
than the old women:

> I remember a warm kitchen on a stormy winter night. I am sitting on
> the floor with my Cheechum and the old ladies. The room is full of
> grandpas, mammas and papas, aunties, uncles and cousins. There is
> laughter, hot sweet tea and the smell of red willow tobacco. "Hahaa
> kiyas mana kisayanoo kah kee achimoot ... Long ago the old man told
> us this story," my uncle would begin and my Cheechum and the old
> ladies would puff their clay pipes and nod. "Tapwe anima, tapwe ... Yes,
> yes it is true."
> ... Today, the stories I heard then, I have learned, and I have been
> given permission to share them with you. They are old men's stories. I
> had hoped when I became a student of storytelling that I would get old
> women teachers, but that was not meant to be. The old women were
> kind, made me pots of tea, cooked me soup and bannock, made me
> starblankets and moccasins, then sent me off to the old men who be-
> came my teachers. (1995, 2)

As in Campbell's case, Elders will direct the learning process for those
who ask, often doing so in a traditional way. They seem to know what
the learner is capable of absorbing. They connect the learner with the
teacher who is most appropriate for the learner or for the type of knowledge being sought. The learner needs to have faith and trust in the
Elders who are directing the learning process and needs to follow their
lead.

Maria Campbell carries out her cultural responsibility of sharing her
learning and takes ownership of any mistakes. This is a gentle reminder
to me that I should also take responsibility for any mistakes contained
in my research because those who shared their knowledge with me did
so with great care and often said that they spoke the truth as they knew
it. Another important principle of learning through storytelling is that
since stories can be heard again and again, the meanings that one makes
or doesn't make from them can happen at any time. One does not have

to give a meaning right after hearing a story, as with the question-and-answer pedagogical approach. An important consideration is hearing stories over time so that they become embedded in memory.

> With the stories, I have had lifetimes of "stuff" put into my memory. I am not even sure what it all is but the teachers say, "Don't worry about it, just think that your brain is the computer you use and we are the people typing it in. When you need it, or you have had the experience to understand it, your spirit will give it to you." I have learned to trust them. It is in this spirit that I share these stories with you. I give them to you in the dialect and rhythm of my village and my father's generation. I am responsible for all the mistakes. (1995, 2)

A similar "timeless" experience was shared by Simon Ortiz, of the Acoma Pueblo, New Mexico, who strongly connected to stories heard in his childhood but did not recognize their communal power until he was older: "All were interesting and vitally important to me because, I could not explain it then, they tied me into the communal body of my people and heritage." By using English and writing, he found new ways to ensure that these stories would continue: "Consequently, when I learned to read and write, I believe I felt those stories continued somehow in the new language and use of the new language and they would never be lost, forgotten, and finally gone. They would always continue" (1992, 9). Like numerous Elders before him, Ortiz learned to use English and writing as "tools" to represent the orally told stories. The oral tradition of the stories shaped and created a framework in which to place and use literacy. Transforming the orally told stories to another language and another form of representation so that the power and integrity of the stories remains requires that one know the essential characteristics of stories. I have heard Elders talk about the necessity of knowing the "core" of the stories. I believe that this means knowing the basic content of the story, the story genre's characteristics or nature, as well as the cultural teachings connected to the story.

Principles for Creating Story Meaning

Simon Ortiz reminds us of how the oral tradition reflects the belief system and consciousness of a people.

> The oral tradition of Native American people is based upon spoken language, but it is more than that too. Oral tradition is inclusive; it is

the actions, behavior, relationships, practices throughout the whole social, economic, and spiritual life process of people. In this respect, the oral tradition is the consciousness of the people. I think at times "oral tradition" is defined too strictly in terms of verbal-vocal manifestations in stories, songs, meditations, ceremonies, ritual, philosophies, and clan and tribal histories passed from older generations to the next ... Oral tradition evokes and expresses a belief system. (1992, 7)

Learning how a story fits within a people's belief system requires that one live with or interact with the people for a long time. The communal principle of storytelling implies that a listener is or becomes a member of the community. Lee Maracle, of the Stó:lō/Coast Salish Nation, reinforces the communal spiritual reverence of oratory:

Oratory: place of prayer, to persuade. This is a word we can work with. We regard words as coming from original being – a sacred spiritual being. The orator is coming from a place of prayer and as such attempts to be persuasive. Words are not objects to be wasted. They represent the accumulated knowledge, cultural values, the vision of an entire people or peoples. We believe the proof of a thing or idea is in the doing. Doing requires some form of social interaction and thus, story is the most persuasive and sensible way to present the accumulated thoughts and values of a people. (1992, 87)

Using the written English language to portray a story can be very problematic to Aboriginal storytellers because its framework (principles, values, and format) may be very different from the Aboriginal framework. Maria Campbell had to understand the Métis communication structure of her community before she presented her people's stories in the English language. She also had to understand how the English language and its writing structure overshadowed Métis ways of communicating a story and learn to manipulate the English language/structure in order to tell a Métis story in a Métis way:

For a long time I couldn't write anything, because I didn't know how to use English. I'm articulate in English. I know it well. But when I was writing I always found that English manipulated me. Once I understood my own rhythms, the language of my people, the history of storytelling, and the responsibility of storytelling, then I was able to manipulate the language. And once I started to be able to manipulate English, I felt that was personal liberation. (Campbell et al. 1992, 9-10)

The personal liberation that Campbell speaks of is linked to communal responsibility. Jeannette Armstrong, of the Okanagan Nation, speaks about a way of listening as preparation for taking responsibility for the effect on others of one's words/thoughts when shared publicly:

One of the central instructions to my people is to practise quietness, to listen, and speak only if you know the full meaning of what you say. It is said that you cannot call your words back once they are uttered, and so you are responsible for all which results from your words. It is said that, for those reasons, it is best to prepare very seriously and carefully to make public contributions. (Armstrong and Cardinal 1991, 90)

The storyteller's responsibility toward others is linked to the power that her/his stories may have. Leslie Marmon Silko speaks of the Laguna Pueblo's communal concept of the healing power and influence of story:

The old folks said the stories themselves had the power to protect us and even to heal us because the stories are alive; the stories are our ancestors. In the very telling of the stories, the spirits of our beloved ancestors and family become present with us. The ancestors love us and care for us though we may not know this. (1996, 152)

Remembering the stories is important not only for continuing the oral tradition but also to help one continue in a healthy way: "The old-time people always say, remember the stories, the stories will help you be strong" (71). The term "remember" implies that one may, if given the authority, tell the stories to others, thereby practising the principle of reciprocity.

Nora Marks Dauenhauer, of the Tlingit Nation of Juneau, Alaska, describes a culture-specific principle of reciprocity embedded in Tlingit oral tradition and culture to show its multidimensional meaning of

ownership and reciprocity. Songs, stories, artistic designs, personal names, land use and other elements of Tlingit are considered the real property of a particular clan. The Tlingit name for this concept is at.óow.

The form, content, and immediate setting of oral tradition exist in a larger context of reciprocity or "balance." The form and content of verbal and visual art are congruent with each other and with social structure.

The two moieties, Eagle and Raven, balance each other out. They select marriage partners from each other, and direct love songs and most oratory to each other. In host-guest relationships at feasts, they share in each other's joy and work to remove each other's grief. This balancing is reflected in the oral literature itself.

Here are some examples:

1) Ravens and Eagles address each other.
2) A song or speech must be answered – not in competition, but that it be received and not "wander aimlessly." (Dauenhauer 1986, 105-6)

Collaborating: Between People, between Languages

Some First Nations people use a collaborative approach to provide cultural information about the principles or the "core" of First Nations stories and/or to present stories in an Aboriginal language and/or to transform it into English. Their collaborations show the interrelatedness principle at work.

Younger First Nations people are collaborating with Elders to publish culture-specific stories. Darwin Hanna and Mamie Henry (1995), of the Nlha7kapmx Nation, edited the book *Our telling: Interior Salish stories of the Nlha7kapmx people.* Darwin is a UBC law school graduate and Mamie is an Elder who teaches the Nhla7kapmx language at Lytton, British Columbia. They visited Elders in their cultural territory and asked them to share their stories, which many did, often telling their stories in the Nlha7kapmx language. The stories were transcribed, translated, and checked by Nlha7kapmx-language speakers from their community. Very little editing was done in order to retain the storytellers' personalities in the literate version.

Darwin Hanna notes that the stories that were translated from Nlha7kapmx into English are more "polished" and seem to flow more "smoothly" than the stories told in English. He attributes this difference to "how one sounds when speaking a language with which one is not completely comfortable" (15). I also noticed that the translated stories had more detail than those told in English.

In the book's "Afterword," the chief and councillors of the Cook's Ferry Band, of which Darwin is a member, affirmed their and the band members' support for the research and publication process. Respect toward the Elders and their cultural knowledge was their prime concern. Because of Darwin's work history, they knew that "the stories would be recorded properly and that the elders would be treated with respect" (201). It is rare to find such support from one's own cultural community printed in a publication. The band council also voiced its responsibility for cultural knowledge:

> The most important qualities of our culture are our language and our stories. In [an] oral tradition such as ours, telling stories is how we pass on the history and teachings of our ancestors. Without these stories, we would have to rely on other people for guidance and information about our past. Teachings in the form of stories are an integral part of our identity as a people and as a nation. If we lose these stories, we will do a disservice to our ancestors – those who gave us the responsibility to keep our culture alive. (201)

Another example of respectful story research is that of Freda Ahenakew, a Cree associate professor of Native studies, and H.C. Wolfart, a non-Native professor of linguistics, who co-edited a book of reminiscences and personal stories told by seven elderly Cree women: *Our grandmothers' lives as told in their own words*. The women spoke in the Cree language to Freda Ahenakew. The grandmothers' stories were translated and written as told with no "smoothing over" and with care similar to that described by Hanna and Henry. Fidelity to the Cree language was an important feature of their approach in order to ensure an accurate representation of the Elders' knowledge.

> In presenting the original Cree texts – in both roman and syllabic orthography and accompanied by a careful translation into English – told by seven women, we want to make sure that they are heard speaking to us in their own words. (1992, "Preface")

Those who speak and read Cree have the benefit of seeing a traditional form of orality, in its original language. I have heard many Aboriginal language speakers say that so much cultural meaning and humour is lost in the translation into the English language. Some of the Cree women who shared their stories have now passed to the Spirit World, but their values, messages, and history in their own words and language will live on.

The transformation of the Indigenous oral language into printed text, in both the Indigenous language and English, not only has the challenge of ensuring the accuracy of content and meaning from one language to another, but also has to maintain the spirit of the oral tradition. An example of a text that does this is Nora Marks Dauenhauer and Richard Dauenhauer's co-edited *Haa tuwunaagu yis, for healing our spirit: Tlingit oratory.* The editors are a married couple and a "professional collaborative team" (1990, ix); Nora Marks Dauenhauer is a member of the Tlingit Nation, Alaska, and her non-Native husband has a background in language and literature. The Dauenhauers worked with eighteen Elders, first recording their speeches in the Tlingit language and then, with their verification, translating them into the English language. The book is structured so that pertinent introductory ethnographic information on Tlingit culture, important themes, types, and structures of orality, and biographies and pictures of the Elders are sequentially combined to aid the reader's acquaintance with and learning of Tlingit oratory. All the speeches are printed in the Tlingit and English languages, and a Tlingit-English glossary is provided. The editors discuss their ethics and the purpose of their work:

> We see this book as a Tlingit book; it belongs ultimately to the Tlingit people and to the clans involved. The speeches in Tlingit are the words of the elders themselves, as they spoke them. We have tried to present their words in English through careful translation, and we have tried to bring additional meaning to them through commentary in the introduction, annotations, and biographies. The oratory presented here has been documented for our children and for all younger generations in the Tlingit community that they may come to a greater understanding of and an appreciation for their heritage and traditions.
>
> As editors, we are salaried to do this work, but we make no money from the sale of books ... royalties normally accruing to the editors will go to Sealaska Heritage Foundation to be used for the publication of additional books "lifting up" the elders to whom the work is dedicated, honoring their achievement and their memories. (xxxv)

The Dauenhauers have carefully spoken through a written form to share Elders' important speech and teachings for the benefit of Tlingit people. This book and process of bringing together an Indigenous culture and ethnography could serve as a model for bringing together epistemology and research methodology. The introductory ethnographic information helps the cultural "outsider" gain some contextual background to understanding the meanings in the Elders' orality. If one does not know the cultural values and "codes," then an understanding of the oral tradition may not occur.

At the same time, ethnographic information has some real limits. The Ojibway writer Armand Ruffo explains a limitation of ethnography that has strongly influenced my thinking. In his analysis of the story "Tracks," written by American Indian writer Louise Erdrich, Ruffo asks these questions: "How much goes unnoticed? How much is left unknown? How much can the 'outsider' really know and feel?" (1993, 163). Neither ethnographic detail, no matter how "rich and thick," nor ethnographic interpretation, no matter how close to "truth," can replace living with the people and being "initiated" into their cultural community. In Erdrich's story the hunter Eli is helped by the vision of an Elder man, Nanapush, while on a winter moose-hunting journey. Eli performs a ceremony after he kills a moose. For the long walk home, Eli cuts pieces of the moose and ties them to parts of his body, enabling him to carry much of the animal. The meat freezes to Eli's outer garments and assumes his body's shape. Ruffo makes this point:

> For the outsider, then, attempting to come to terms with Native people and their literature, the problem is not one to be solved by merely attaining the necessary background, reading all the anthropological data that one can get one's hands on. Rather, for those who are serious, it is more a question of cultural initiation, of involvement and commitment, so that the culture and literature itself becomes more than a mere museum piece, dusty pages, something lifeless. Think of Eli, after his kill, wrapped in moose meat; in Nanapush's words "the moose is transformed into the mold of Eli, an armor that would fit no other." That is how Native culture should fit if one is truly to understand its literature [stories] and people. (174)

In reflecting on Ruffo's words, I experienced a deep personal connection with his point of view. My criticism of enthnography's limitations is not aimed at the ethnographer. My point is that, at most, the reader can glean an introduction to Aboriginal culture and oral tradition through ethnography, even if presented as well as that of the Dauenhauers. If the reader wants to gain an understanding of the oral tradition, she/he cannot be a passive observer or armchair reader. According to Ruffo, the oral tradition "implicates the 'listener' [reader] into becoming an active participant in the experience of the story" (164). An interrelationship between the story, storytelling, and listener is another critical principle of storywork.

Interrelatedness between Story and Listener and between Text and Reader

> Mabel once said: "Don't ask me what it means, the story. Life will teach you about it, the way it teaches you about life." It is important that I remember my life, my presence and history, as I attempt to understand Mabel. As I learn more about Mabel, I learn more about myself. In this way, using much of what Mabel has taught me, I show in these essays myself and others learning, seeing beyond what things seem to be. I chart dialogues that open and explore interpersonal and intercultural territories. (Sarris 1993, 5)

In *Keeping Slug Woman alive*, Greg Sarris (1993), of the Kasha Pomo Nation, invites the reader to interact with his many stories. He shares his interactions and critical thoughts about making meaning from the late Mabel McKay's stories and talks. Mabel McKay was a Cache Creek Pomo medicine woman from the Santa Rosa area of California and Sarris's relative, from whom he learned over a thirty-year period. Sarris provides the reader with a framework for thinking critically about one's own historical, cultural, and current context in relation to the story being told by using his personal life-experience stories as examples. He advocates this kind of synergy between the story, or text, and the reader's life experience.

Sarris also cautions Indigenous people about using textual frameworks that are acceptable in academe but that result in disrespectful representations, or make us the objective "Other," or create opportunities for sacred knowledge to be appropriated:

> In creating narratives for others about our histories and religions, in what ways are we not only compromising those histories and religions but at the same time compromising our identities, that are largely dependent upon these, as well as our resistance to the colonizer and dominant culture? (68)

The critical interactive relationship between the reader and text that he advocates is the opposite of what he and countless others, including myself, experienced in university classrooms through the "objective textual" presentation of Indian cultures and people:

> Though I could not articulate my feeling at the time, I sensed what bothered me when reading "Indian books" for "Indian courses" at the university. Objectivism and text positivism, which influenced pedagogical practices at the time, hardly encouraged readers to think of people and places outside the actual text. I was not encouraged to engage my personal experience as I was at home when hearing stories. The text was supposedly complete, self-contained, a thing to dissect rather than to have a relationship with. (186)

Gerald Vizenor also believes that the story listener must become a participant who is actively engaged with the story:

> The story doesn't work without a participant ... there has to be a participant and someone has to listen. I don't mean listening in the passive sense. You can even listen by contradiction ... So that's really critical in storytelling. (1987, 300-1)

Synergistic interaction between storyteller, listener, and story is another critical storywork principle.

The literature presented in this chapter introduces some facets of the storywork principles of respect, responsibility, reciprocity, reverence, holism, interrelatedness, and synergy. I have used Coyote's new eyes to identify these principles with the help of the experienced Indigenous storytellers mentioned above. These principles will be the "markers" along the trails that Coyote takes us on as we continue our travels and as we learn more about storywork in the chapters that follow.

CHAPTER TWO

Coyote Searching for the Bone Needle

As I think about research in relation to Indigenous peoples, I remember a story that Eber Hampton, of the Chickasaw Nation, told about a particular Trickster. After telling the story, he talked about the connections between motives and methods in research. This story has stayed in my memory and has become a more integral part of my being with each telling. Every time I tell a story, I acknowledge the storyteller and/or source of the story. The traditional stories that I tell are ones given to me or ones published by a storyteller. Eventually, Eber gave me permission to use the story "Coyote Searching for the Bone Needle" with the encouragement to adapt it to suit my cultural context. I renamed the Trickster Old Man Coyote because Coyote in all his/her/its forms has become my Trickster of learning.

COYOTE SEARCHING FOR THE BONE NEEDLE

Old Man Coyote had just finished a long hard day of hunting. He decided to set up his camp for the night. After supper, he sat by the fire and rubbed his tired feet from the long day's walk. He took his favourite moccasins out of his bag and noticed that there was a hole in the toe of one of them. He looked for his special bone needle to mend the moccasin but couldn't feel it in the bag.

Old Man Coyote started to crawl on his hands and knees around the fire to see if

he could see or feel the needle. Just then Owl came flying
by and landed next to Old Man Coyote. He asked him
what he was looking for. Old Man Coyote told Owl his
problem.

Owl said that he would help his friend look for the bone
needle. After he made one swoop around the area of the
fire, he told Old Man Coyote that he didn't see the needle.
Owl said that if it were around the fire, then he would
have spotted it. He then asked Old Man Coyote where he
last used the needle. Old Man Coyote said that he used it
quite far away, over in the bushes, to mend his jacket.

Then Owl asked Old Man Coyote why he was searching
for the needle around the campfire. Old Man Coyote
replied, "Well, it's easier to look for the needle here because
the fire gives off such good light, and I can see better here."

In my search for a culturally appropriate Indigenous research methodology – a bone needle – about Indigenous storytelling, I started with
the principles of respect for cultural knowledge embedded in the stories
and respect for the people who owned or shared stories as an ethical
guide. Like Old Man Coyote I wanted the (re)search to be easy. I didn't
really want to deal with colonial history, and I did not want to question
my motives and methods. But unlike Old Man Coyote, I knew that I
had to venture to the unfamiliar territory of decolonization by questioning my motives and methods and ensuring that the negative legacy
of research history was addressed. I asked myself, "Was I doing anything different from earlier 'outsider' academics who created a legacy of
mistrust among First Nations concerning academic research?" "How was
my research going to benefit the education and wellbeing of Indigenous
peoples and their communities?" "How would I address ethical issues
related to respect and ownership of Indigenous intellectual property?"
Ignoring or remaining mired in collective colonized history is like staying near the fire. Going away from the fire and finding ways to move
beyond the history of colonization is hard but necessary work. Staying
near the fire and trying to adapt qualitative methodology to fit an Indigenous oral tradition is also problematic because Indigenous theory
does not drive the methodology. Finally, I figured out that in order to
find an Indigenous methodology and address the aforementioned questions, I had to go back to the Elders. I had to learn about Stó:lō story
principles in order to find Stó:lō story theory. My journey of going back

to the Stó:lō Elders was like going into the dark, even though I knew the Elders. What I didn't know was how to work with story within a framework that provided both theoretical and practical Indigenous guidance for research and education.

Taking Direction from Elders

From my understanding of First Nations cultural ways, authority and respect are attributed to "Elders" – people who have acquired wisdom through life experiences, education (a process of gaining skills, knowledge, and understanding), and reflection. Elder Dr. Ellen White, of the Snuneymuxw Coast Salish Nation, said this about Elder characteristics: "To be an elder you first have to be accepted, listened to, and not laughed at. You have to be a good speaker ... You always know where it's [knowledge] going to be in your memory, in your mind. It's so easy to just go into that – they always mention a basket [metaphor] and you know it's all in there" (quoted in Neel 1992, 107). Elder Beatrice Medicine, of the Lakota/Sioux Nation, says: "Elders are repositories of cultural and philosophical knowledge and are the transmitters of such information" (1987, 142). Age is not a factor in one's becoming an Elder. As noted in Ellen White's definition, being respected by others and having cultural knowledge are critical criteria. Elders have varying knowledges, or "gifts," to pass on to others, whether spiritual, healing, medicinal, historical, storytelling, or linguistic.

Important cultural knowledge and teachings are learned carefully – over time – through interaction with Elder teachers. A researcher who enters a First Nations cultural context with little or no cultural knowledge is viewed as a learner. Entering a learner-teacher relationship requires time and the practice of various cultural protocols before teaching and learning can really occur. I have heard many Elders say that they wait to be asked to share their knowledge. The term "share" implies teaching. If a learner is really serious about learning in a traditional manner, then the learner must ask and must make her/himself culturally ready, perhaps through "protocol," to receive the knowledge. Walter Lightning describes the term "protocol":

That term, protocol, refers to any one of a number of culturally ordained actions and statements, established by ancient tradition that an individual completes to establish a relationship with another person from whom the individual makes a request. The protocols differ according to the nature of the request and the nature of the individuals involved. The actions and statements may be outwardly simple and straightforward, or they may be complex, involving preparation lasting a year or more. The protocols may often involve the presentation of something. It would be a mistake to say that what is presented is symbolic of whatever may be requested, or the relationship that it is hoped will be established, because it is much more than symbolic. (1992, 216)

If researchers don't follow cultural protocol and don't take the necessary time to develop respectful relationships with Elder teachers, but instead begin to pose questions, they may find that the teachers answer the questions indirectly or not at all. When this happens the role of researchers as outside "research experts" ought to quickly change to one of "research and cultural learners." They must begin their job by getting to know the teachers and by learning to listen and watch before engaging in the challenge of making meaning and gaining understanding from the Elders' talks and actions. Researchers need to learn and to appreciate the form and process of teacher-learner protocol, the form of communication, and the social principles and practices embedded in the First Nations cultural context. None of these steps is easy, quick, or simple.

Through this inquiry/learning process, the questions of the researchers, now learners, may change depending on the context and what they need to know and can understand. The end result is that the skills, knowledge, understanding, and perhaps insight gained over a lengthy period must be shared with others in a manner that incorporates cultural respect, responsibility, reciprocity, and reverence. The voices of the teachers, their knowledge, and the way that this knowledge is represented and publicly shared must be in compliance with culturally "proper" ways. For example, particular stories must be told accurately – as "handed down" – and not told unless the storyteller, who must always be acknowledged, grants permission. Some stories may not be told during particular times of the year.

Three Elders, Simon Baker, Vincent Stogan, and Ellen White, taught me important research lessons. Through their teachings and the confidence that they shared in me, Simon, Vincent, and Ellen prepared me for undertaking storywork as an Indigenous methodology.

Chief Khot-La-Cha, Dr. Simon Baker

I first met Dr. Simon Baker in 1985, but I knew about him for many more years in his role as Chief of his reserve, speaker for the Squamish people, and ambassador for First Nations. When I became the supervisor of the Native Indian Teacher Education Program (NITEP) at the University of British Columbia, our group invited Simon Baker to speak to students on many occasions. He eventually became our NITEP Elder. Simon's humour and life-experience stories about cultural, political, social, and economic survival are ways that he carried out his Elder teaching responsibilities. My relationship with Simon took on a different teaching and learning dimension when he became one of my research advisors.

I invited Simon to breakfast one day in the winter of 1990. We talked for quite a while. He spoke about his life experiences. He always talked about his ancestors and what they had taught him. I talked to Simon Baker many times for research, educational, and personal purposes between 1990 and his death in 2001. In the earlier years, I voiced my concerns about story representation and appropriation of stories. He helped me appreciate the cultural concept of reciprocity. He also helped me understand how to pilot an interview and how to conduct its analysis in the beginning stages of the research process.

Simon's persistence in mentoring others and in ensuring that First Nations cultural knowledge and values continue has helped me deal with "guilt" feelings associated with academic research. They don't disappear, but they don't stop me from making space in academe to deal with ethical issues and actions. Simon's later years of life were devoted to sharing and teaching cultural knowledge that brought healing and good life to people. I have come to believe that bringing together cultural knowledge and research can create a better life for us and future generations.

Even though I am a First Nations person and have some initial understandings about various First Nations cultures, I became like an outsider when I began to use the "tools" of literacy to record my research observations and reflections about the oral traditions and practices through fieldnotes and now in this book:

> I felt tension in doing my first ethnographic observations at an Elders' gathering for a fieldnote exercise. Tension/uneasiness because I had to record people's behaviours, their words in key phrases, the physical setting, the chronological order of events, which is antithetical to the way I normally participate in this type of cultural gathering. Even if I hadn't taken notes during the event, I viewed everything with different eyes. Tension/anxiety because I had to become and see like an outsider.

To do this, I visualized the event within a circle, and I stood outside it and I looked in. The act of writing notes also made me feel like an outsider. Tension/resistance because I knew I would be eventually writing for others about what I had seen and interpreted, thus transforming myself and culture. (Journal entries, 27 May, 20 June, 5 July 1991)

I am also a university academic, which again may place me on the borders of First Nations contexts. First Nations people are encouraged by Elders and local community to "get more education." But becoming educated in mainstream institutions can create a chasm between the person who is university-educated and others who are not educated in this way. The critical rational thinking, questioning, and writing required by academe is like one of the mismatched eyes that Coyote acquires in the story recounted in Chapter 1. A First Nations way of thinking and communicating may be the other eye. Being university-educated, I have to work hard at showing others of my community that I still share their cultural values and that I am still at heart a First Nations person – that I have some form of harmony and balance.

I have learned to use either eye when necessary. Many Elders have said many times that one must learn to "live in two worlds." This metaphoric statement still holds true today, even though there are more "worlds"; there are various academic, social, political, and cultural milieux in which one may find oneself today. The words of Elder Ellen White help soothe the uneasy feelings:

To young people my grandparents always said, "You'll do all right if your hands are both full to overflowing." One hand could be filled with the knowledge of the White man and the other could be filled with the knowledge of your ancestors. You could study the ancestors, but without a deep feeling of communication with them it would be surface learning and surface talking. Once you have gone into yourself and have learnt very deeply, appreciate it, and relate to it very well, everything will come very easily. They always said that if you have the tools of your ancestors and you have the tools of the White man, his speech, his knowledge, his ways, his courts, his government, you'll be able to deal with a lot of things at his level. You'll not be afraid to say anything you want. A lot of people keep back – they say, "Oh, I might hurt them – I might say something." When your hands are both full with the knowledge of both sides, you'll grow up to be a great speaker, great organizer, great doer, and a helper of your people. (Quoted in Neel 1992, 108)

Some of my uneasiness is based on the educational and employment inequities faced by Indigenous people who truly possess cultural knowledge. I benefit from this research work by completing a book, which enhances my career. Many of our Elders and cultural people are not given due recognition (i.e., equality of pay) in educational institutions for their depth of cultural knowledge. During one of my conversations with Simon Baker, I brought up a suggestion concerning possible publication of a book. I suggested that if a book were to occur from the research work, then any monies received from sales would go to an Elders' fund. Even though sales of educational books do not result in a lot of money for the author, some financial reciprocity would occur. He thought that this was a good idea and also talked about another ethical issue, that of appropriation, noting a time when someone used his words and knowledge without acknowledgment:

> In my den, I have many tapes in there. A lot of them say "Why don't you let us use it?" I say, "No, unless you people invite me or do something. I'll be glad to do it. But I'm not going to give you what I got so you can write and use it, and say I did this." That's what [so and so] did to me. Oh [so and so] sure used me. I don't mind it if you come, like you did, that's when I give you permission, that's good. I respect you for that, and I know a lot of it will come out for good use. That's very good. (Transcript, 18 February 1992)

I am very honoured that Chief Simon Baker agreed to be my guide and teacher. My talks with him eased my anxiety. I came to realize that respect must be an integral part of the relationship between the Elder and the researcher – respect for each other as human beings, respect for the power of cultural knowledge, and respect for cultural protocols that show one's honour for the authority and expertise of the Elder teacher.

The principle of respect includes trust and being culturally worthy. Floy Pepper, an Elder of the Choctaw Nation, who is one of my mentors, read an earlier draft of this book and told me that she was tired of reading about my anxious feelings. She thought I meant that I did not feel worthy and ready to receive the Elders' cultural knowledge and teachings. Upon reflection, I had to agree that not feeling culturally ready or culturally worthy was another dimension of the complex ethical feelings that I experienced. Now, I understand that being culturally worthy means being ready intellectually, emotionally, physically, and spiritually to fully absorb cultural knowledge. Getting ready in this holistic way is like participating in the cultural protocol that Walter Lightning describes.[1]

In addition, the researcher must trust and have patience that the Elder is guiding the learning process in a culturally appropriate way. The Elder must also be culturally trustworthy. Some Aboriginal people who mistakenly have been called Elders have also been accused of sexual abuse. When I talk about trust, I don't mean that one should have "blind" trust, only that one must know when an Elder is worthy of trust and respect. In the background, I hear Coyote asking for the easy answer to how one knows.

I also want to transform my anxiety into positive action and begin to make systemic change so that learning institutions such as schools, colleges, and universities appropriately recognize and provide compensation for the knowledge expertise of Elders and cultural teachers.

Telling Stories as a Way of Interviewing

I believe that sources of fundamental and important Indigenous knowledge are the land, our spiritual beliefs and ceremonies, traditional teachings of Elders, dreams, and our stories. In seeking to understand Elders' teachings, knowing the values and actions of responsibility, respect, reverence, and reciprocity are essential. Thomas King, a Cherokee storyteller, offers an explanation of a traditional teaching about "all my relations" that exemplifies these values:

> "All my relations" is at first a reminder of who we are and of our relationship with both our family and our relatives. It also reminds us of the extended relationship we share with all human beings. But the relationships that Native people see go further, the web of kinship extending to the animals, to the birds, to the fish, to the plants, to all the animate and inanimate forms that can be seen or imagined. More that that, "all my relations" is an encouragement for us to accept the responsibilities we have within this universal family by living our lives in a harmonious and moral manner (a common admonishment is to say of someone that they act as if they have no relations). (1990, ix)

I believe that understandings and insights also result from lived experiences and critical reflections on those experiences. Many Aboriginal people have said that to understand ourselves and our situation today, we must know where we come from and know what has influenced us. The historical and intergenerational effects of colonization and assimilation still affect our people and communities today. Elders' life stories can show how we, as Indigenous peoples, survived and how we can keep our cultural knowledges intact. Their life stories depict resilience and resistance to colonization.

At first, I used a reflexive interview approach, as discussed by Hammersley and Atkinson (1983); that is, I used issues rather than a list of questions to guide the process. There were issues that bothered me, and I wanted some general direction in which to guide the initial research process. I wanted to ask Simon's advice on whom I might approach and how I should start my research work. I also needed to discuss ways of getting people to work with me and to discuss ethical concerns about research.

Analyzing the Transcript

My beginning interview/talk with Simon Baker helped me understand how to work with an Elder's talk. Before transcribing the tape, I thought about the teachings that Simon wanted me to learn. I listened to the tape twice. He talked a lot about Elders, how important it is to go to them, to listen to what they have to say, and to show respect by spending time with them in order to establish a learning relationship. One answer to my question of who to work with was Elders. During his talk, he stressed the importance of living honourably and showing respect to everyone, even if you dislike a person. In time, this respect could be returned to you. It was after this talk that I decided to seek out those Elders who continue to practise and pass on their cultural teachings.

Simon also made me realize the importance of keeping the tapes and perhaps finding a way to have them available so that others can hear and appreciate the Elders' way of talking and the knowledge shared. The tapes serve as a record of cultural history, along with the written talks. However, sometimes the person who is talking names others and may talk about experiences that are of a confidential nature because of the trust and ease established in the research/learning relationship. Then the tapes may not be ethically shared. Permission would also need to be given to use the tapes for purposes other than this book.

Responsible story use is important, yet it is also complex, making it difficult to understand and carry out. Thomas King powerfully articulates this complexity: "Stories are wondrous things. And they are dangerous" (2003, 9). I have found that going back each time for permission to use tapes, quotations, or stories for purposes other than those initially agreed upon is regarded as a "nuisance" by the person who generated the knowledge. There can be an implied understanding that once permission is given and trust is established, the knowledge can be used for teaching and learning purposes as long as proper acknowledgment of the source is made clear and the knowledge is used responsibly.

Giving and getting permission raises ethical questions of who has authority to give permission and under what circumstances. The researcher given permission has the ethical responsibility to understand the limits of permission and try to prevent her/his abuse of the knowledge and permission. Sometimes institutional procedures, such as making people sign documents and continually asking them to check the written versions for accuracy, may create an atmosphere of distrust or the impresssion that the learner/researcher can't get it right. The importance of establishing a teaching-learning research relationship based on trust and ethical responsibility became more important to me in the work with Simon Baker and others.

Eisner Mishler's (1986) notion of the interview as a speech event facilitating the creation of narratives and the cultural relationship between teacher and learner was evident in this particular transcript. The quantity of what I say is much less than what Simon says. I feel that Elders should be given as much time as they need and want to talk. Some Elders like to talk at length and may seem to get off topic, but I've learned that there is usually a reason for the stories that they share. In research situations, their expertise should be respected, and it is the researchers' responsibility to make meaning from what they say. If the Elders fully understand and are committed to the importance of research "work," they will say what is necessary.

With Simon's talk, I tried to note the start of new stories that he told throughout the transcript because I wondered whether the stories could be categorized into various types. This was hard to do. Simon told many stories, and it was not clear whether a story was completely finished before he started on a new one. He described survival activities that he experienced with his grandmother and uncles, the teachings of various Elders, and his current lifestyle in relation to the past. Many different life experiences were brought together to make a composite story of his life. The themes that were repeated and that stood out were knowledge from nature, learning by listening, Elders' ways of teaching, Elders' responsibility and time for reflection, living right, and the responsibility of the learner to seek out and question the Elders.

When I listened to the tape and heard my "talk," I was embarrassed by my ramblings and hesitations, which dealt with my guilt about ethical issues. Toward the end of the interview, Simon mentioned the traditional way of speaking. I really wanted him to continue because I was interested in the structure and content of speaking. However, I realized that we had been sitting for a long time and that Simon was tired. I also knew that we would continue our discussions over a long period.

After taking Simon back to his home, I recalled the healing emotions that I had felt during the interview. He had provided me with good things to think about. He had soothed my anxiety. He had also pointed out some markers that I could place on my "journeying" map that would act as "bearings" to help me find my way as I began to explore the territory of First Nations orality. When my research advisor, Celia Haig-Brown, read my initial fieldnotes and transcript, she wondered why Simon hadn't answered my questions. She asked me to say more about why I felt "good" after the talk because she didn't understand the flow of the stories. She voiced her concern about my lack of critical engagement with the transcript. In response, I wrote this fieldnote to her and to me:

If Simon Baker talks more about his life experiences, and does not appear to be answering my questions, then why? If I am to work with Elders such as Simon, then I will probably have experiences similar to the one evident in the transcript. Therefore, I need to see what I can learn from the process of analysis, which should make me go back – think back to the process of "interviewing" or having a talk. The following questions could be possibilities to probe:

1 Are my questions clearly stated? Does he understand them? I could try asking them again another time, without the tentativeness evident the first time.

2 Am I asking the wrong questions at this particular time? Should I take more time to establish a teacher-learner relationship with him? I know Simon quite well, but I have not worked with him on this particular topic or area in depth. Perhaps his life story is a way for me to get to know him more (how he was raised, what teachings are important to him, how he views the world – what and who has shaped his worldview). If I spend more time with Simon, he will also get to know me better, and to understand what my learning needs are, in a

way to make him become a traditional teacher, similar to how he describes his relationship with his grandmother.

3 Does Simon have his own purpose for the stories he tells? Remember Julie Cruikshank's experience where the three Yukon First Nations Elders politely evaded answering her questions, and told her stories instead? As Julie worked with the Elders, they took increasing control of the research process. However, Julie came to see the women's ways of telling stories as a way of telling her about themselves and their histories. It seems they all had a similar purpose – to record history, but each wanted to achieve it in different ways: Julie at first wanted to hear and record chronicled events, while the women wanted to tell traditional kinds of stories. It would appear that Julie decided to honour the Elders' ways of telling their stories – and to honour their ways of knowing.

... Or perhaps I have to learn which of Simon's words should stay inside my mind and which ones should "go out the other ear," as he has said. Having a transcript allows me to go back over the words, to pick ones for particular meanings at this stage of my thinking and research, and to leave the others, which can be revisited later.

Perhaps in my initial analysis I focused on trying to see what themes or messages were contained in each of Simon's stories rather than on seeing how his talk related to the questions asked. Words related to Elders' teachings were highlighted in orange. It appeared that Simon answered the question of who to speak to about stories. He referred to Elders who have traditional teachings and who live respectfully, providing characteristics rather than specific names, and Elders who welcome the opportunity to share their knowledge. Yes, I wondered why he didn't name names. But I know that Simon wants to keep working with me, and perhaps 28 February at the Saskatchewan Restaurant was not the right time or place to get that answer. I have learned from experience with the Stó:lō Elders that an answer may not be evident when a question is first asked. But I have come to understand that when I am ready for and worthy of the answer, it is given. Patience, patience, patience.

Even though Simon may not have said much about the questions regarding reciprocity, I had already given him my answer when I posed the question. I think that I had to admit those guilt feelings to someone like Simon. On page seven of the transcript he tells me that he respects me for the way I came to ask him permission and that he knows "a lot will come out for good use." I guess I wanted to hear that I was doing the right and respectful thing. So what I realize now is that the interview can also be therapeutic for the person posing the questions. (Fieldnote, 31 March 1992)

"Sit down and listen"

Sit down and listen, and that's the thing, our ancestors used to say.
(Chief Simon Baker, transcript, 17 February 1992)

As I continued to work with Simon and learned to "sit down and listen," our talks (interviews) moved from the conventional process, with Simon doing most of the talking, to "research as conversation," then to "research as chat" (Haig-Brown 1992, 104-5), and finally to "research as storytelling." Research as conversation is characterized as an open-ended interview with opportunity for both sides to engage in talk rather than only one party doing most of the talking. Research as chat occurs when the researcher is very familiar with the participant(s) and they interact on a frequent basis.

As I reflect on this process, many years later, I characterize the talking process as one whereby Simon, the Elder, maintained control over what he wanted me to know, but he also was interested in what I thought about various matters and in what issues I was concerned about in my role as director of the First Nations House of Learning at the University of British Columbia (UBC). On many occasions Simon told life-experience stories to illustrate leadership and political strategies that had implications for me – hence research as storytelling. I quit using the tape recorder fairly early on in our research relationship and instead made written and "memory" notes after our discussions. Leilani Holmes defines blood memory and heart knowledge, which is what I experienced in my learning relationship with Chief Khot-La-Cha:

> Knowledge is passed to others in the context of relationships and deep feelings of connection. I have described this as heart knowledge. Knowledge also passes through the generations; thus, Hawaiians are united with the *kupuna* [Elders] of generations past. I have called this knowledge blood memory. (2000, 46)

Tsimilano, Dr. Vincent Stogan

Being in harmony with oneself, others, members of the animal kingdom, and other elements of nature requires that Indigenous people respect the gifts of each entity and establish and maintain respectful reciprocal relations with each. One might ask, how can this principle of cultural respect transcend context and time and be applicable to academic research? I have heard Chief Leonard George of the Tsleil-Waututh First Nation, located on the north shore of Burrard Inlet near North Vancouver, British Columbia, reply to a question with similar implication: "How can urban First Nations maintain their cultures, which may have deep connections to the land, in a city environment?" In answer to this question, he says:

> I try to use old philosophies as a tool. I call it learning how to become a hunter of the city, using the old philosophy of the hunter in the forest and the respect that he had, and using only what you need for that day, and taking it out, bringing it back and sharing it with as many people whose needs will be suited by it. This changed my perspective on the city. It is a wonderful resource then – go in and hunt and get things out and bring it back home. (Quoted in Neel 1992, 53)

What I take from Chief Leonard George's metaphor is that first I need to understand the teachings/values of the "old philosophies," then apply them to my learning in the new environment of Indigenous story research, and then share this learning with others. I exercise this responsibility and reciprocity through this book. Those who are interested in learning about Indigenous research and storywork will find my work and use it appropriately, taking what they need from it. The cycle of reciprocity and reverence toward the spiritual are important dynamics of storywork, which will be shown with the next Elder teacher.

During the process of learning about ethnographic interviewing, I experienced similar lessons about respect, responsibility, and reciprocity between teacher and learner from a respected cultural teacher of the Musqueam people, Dr. Vincent Stogan, whose First Nations name, Tsimilano, means "a great man." I also learned more about the principle of reverence. Vincent Stogan is a spiritual healer and works with many people across Canada and the United States. He and his wife, whom everyone calls "Mom," carry on the traditional healing and spiritual work passed down to him from his relatives:

> A lot of Elders wanted me to take my grandfather's place ... he was a great healer. That old man, he was blind, but he said when I was little ... you are the one that's going to take my place and do this kind of work.

I never thought of it until I was old enough ... I was about forty-five years old I guess when we [Mom and I] noticed that our Elders were going fast, so we made up our mind that we better do the work they want us to do. We put our minds to it and then started the healing work. (Transcript, 16 August 1994)

The spiritual dimension of the holistic paradigm that I presented in Chapter 1 became more evident with my interaction with Elder Vincent Stogan. Because I wanted to explore a topic about which I did not know very much, I approached Vincent Stogan, a respected keeper of the culture. I had known Vincent since 1990, and I watched him work at numerous gatherings until his death in 2000. He was also an Elder advisor to the students, staff, and faculty of the First Nations House of Learning at UBC.

In 1991 Vincent agreed to talk to me about our oral traditions. In our first session, he immediately became the teacher, and I the learner (similar to the relationship between Simon Baker and me). Our teacher-learner relationship was based on respect for Musqueam and Stó:lō cultural ways. Because I am an insider of the culture, I observed a cultural-learning protocol: once he, as the Elder, had determined where we should meet, I ensured that there was sharing of food and tea and created unhurried time and talking space so that we could get to the topic of discussion at the "right" moment. It would have been disrespectful to ask my questions immediately. During breakfast we talked about many things, and I told Vincent about my research interest in the topic of our oral traditions and about the kinds of things that I wanted to know. When he began to talk, he assumed the role of teacher, and I understood that he was agreeing to teach me. His comments show how he intended to direct the learning process:

Another way that I can help you get to know these things, it won't be just like us talking now, it'll take time, I can go just so far and maybe we can carry on some other time ... because this is the teaching that we got that we can't hurry everything ... Well I think knowing you this long, I know your parents now, where you're from, I'm willing to help you. I trust you and I know you're our kind. (Transcript, 17 May 1991)

When Vincent talked about knowing my parents and knowing where I am from, I understood him to mean that our culture bonded us in important ways. He felt responsible for helping me because of this bond.

His decision to help me by becoming my teacher and our subsequent talks made me realize that, as a learner, I too have responsibilities.

Tsimilano's Teaching of Hands Back and Hands Forward

Our relation as teacher and learner had to be based on respect for each other, on respect for the traditional cultural ways of teaching and learning, and on reverence for spirituality. I also realized that reciprocity was essential to our working together. As a learner, I needed to listen carefully and to think "hard" about the meanings in Vincent's personal stories and in his words. I could then check my knowledge and understandings with him to ensure their accuracy. Vincent carried out his Elder responsibility by teaching and also by ensuring the correctness of the learning. My part included acquiring and validating my understandings and eventually sharing them by becoming a teacher to others. This reciprocal action has a cyclical nature that is embedded in the "hands back, hands forward" teaching.

> My dear ones,
>
> Form a circle and join hands in prayer. In joining hands, hold your left palm upward to reach back to grasp the teachings of the ancestors. Put these teachings into your everyday life and pass them on. Hold your right palm downward to pass these teachings on to the younger generation. In this way, the teachings and knowledge of the ancestors continue, and the circle of human understanding and caring grows stronger.

Vincent also carried out important spiritual cultural work. He opened gatherings with prayer and sometimes song. He taught the "younger" ones the spiritual ceremonies. The importance of addressing spiritual needs and asking for spiritual guidance from the Creator became an important teaching for me and continues to guide my work. I have learned that prayer is an essential beginning:

> We always pray first to the Creator ... I think in your kind of work using [spirituality] will help you a lot, it's no shame to pray to the Creator. (Transcript, 17 May 1991)

Until his death Elder Vincent Stogan continued to provide encouragement to me with my story research by teaching me more about traditional spiritual teachings and cultural knowledge. He would phone me or drop by the First Nations Longhouse at UBC to ask how things were going or to say that he and Mom were going travelling. He called me his niece, although we are not directly related by kinship. I stopped taping and interviewing him and followed, for a while, the research-as-chat approach. I then switched to a traditional approach to learning from Tsimilano, learning pieces at a time and not hurrying the learning, as he had first directed me to do. I watched him speak many times and at many different gatherings. We shared many private talks. What he taught me is in my oral memory and an important part of my heart knowledge and my spiritual being. His teachings are reflected on the pages of this book and often guide my interactions with others.

Vincent Stogan also had a significant impact on the work of the First Nations House of Learning at UBC by teaching us the importance of beginning our work, especially events, with prayer. He also opened many of the general university gatherings at UBC with prayer. His prayers, said in the Hen'q'emi'nem language, helped to create a respectful atmosphere in which to interact. He encouraged those in attendance to think their own prayerful or thankful thoughts. This act of prayer was not forced on people, but his thoughts, spoken in his language, signalled a time for caring and connection to the spiritual, to each other, and to oneself. Tsimilano's teachings about the importance of the spiritual in learning continue in various forms throughout many First Nations learning environments today.

Establishing relationships within the context of storywork research has become a way to sustain lasting friendships through deep caring and endless stories and talk. Learning to listen with patience, learning about cultural responsibility toward the oral tradition, learning to make self-understandings, continuing the cycle of reciprocity by sharing cultural knowledge, and practising reverence are some of the lessons that I experienced with Chief Simon Baker and Elder Vincent Stogan. These lessons and others were reinforced through my relationship with Elder Dr. Ellen White, of the Snuneymuxw Coast Salish Nation in Nanaimo, BC, whose First Nations name is Kwulasulwut.

Kwulasulwut, Dr. Ellen White

Kwulasulwut means "many stars." Elder Ellen White became my mentor, teacher, and a dear friend. The collaborative research process that I undertook with Ellen to create an educational journal article highlights some pertinent issues about collaborative analysis of transcripts, editing a text for publication, and considerations for translation from a First

Nations language into English. Working on these issues with Ellen White prepared me for the story-research analysis and verification process with the Stó:lō (Coqualeetza) Elders, which is described in the next chapter.

Establishing a Relationship

I met Dr. Ellen White in 1991, but I knew about her long before that. I have admired Ellen's work as a storyteller, writer, and healer for many years. Her book *Kwulasulwut: Stories from the Coast Salish* gave me inspiration when it was published in 1981 because as a First Nations storyteller and writer, she was able to take the oral traditions that she was taught and put them in a literate form for educational purposes. When I met Ellen at a public lecture at the Museum of Anthropology at UBC, I was struck by her powerful way of passing on her knowledge. Her talk, combined with song, humour, and drumming, engaged the listeners, particularly me. Being there and hearing her words brought me back to the occasions when I listened to the Stó:lō Elders at another time and place. After her talk, I introduced myself and acknowledged her good words, a teaching that I remember Chief Simon Baker encouraging in his many talks. However, this was the first time that I followed his teaching with someone whom I did not personally know. During our short talk, Ellen said that she thought she knew me from other times. I knew intuitively at that moment that I wanted to work with and learn from Ellen. During the summer of 1992 she participated in a working committee to select writings of Aboriginal students for a book about Aboriginal heroes. Our working relationship began with this experience. Ellen also agreed to participate in an educational talk with me about giving voice to our ancestors. This talk was taped, transcribed, co-operatively edited, and printed in the *Canadian Journal of Native Education* (*CJNE*) with Ellen as the lead author (White and Archibald 1992).

We began our work for the *CJNE* article on 18 September 1992. I travelled by ferry to Ellen and her husband Doug's home in Nanaimo. When I arrived, Ellen had made salmon chowder and bannock. As we ate, Doug and I teased each other about who drank the strongest coffee – me from the Stó:lō or him from the Snuneymuxw Coast Salish. In a way, we are related by the Hel'q'emi'nem language. We come from the same cultural traditions. I felt accepted and at home there; I felt like a member of their extended family. Before we began working, I offered Ellen a gift from the First Nations House of Learning to thank her for helping me with this important work.

When Ellen's husband left, I took out the tape recorder, and we sat at the dining room table. I reviewed the intent of the talk, the purpose of *CJNE,* and the process by which we could work together. I would record and transcribe the talk, then review the written transcript with her and get her approval before the text – her story, her words, and her work – was put into written form (similar to the process used by Marcus and Fischer 1986, Wickwire and Robinson 1989, and Cruikshank et al. 1990). Ellen asked what I would add to her words. I said that I wanted to write a reaction to her words and that our article would be co-operative: she and I would be the authors. Ellen said that she liked this approach because I could question what was not clear and add parts that were missing. Then she began talking about some of her ancestors; after a few minutes, she said to turn the tape recorder on.

I remember feeling emotionally strong, spiritually grateful, and intellectually challenged after I left Ellen and Doug White's home. My journal entry reads:

I feel almost overwhelmed! What a rich experience – to be involved at so many layers ... I get immersed in her stories. When Ellen talks about her ancestors, it is as if she is "there with them" – her voice changes and she sounds as if she is her granny. I recall the power of her metaphors: trees, baskets, canoes, hair, paths, air/body. I see these images so vividly and, when I do the comparison, the connection of them to life considerations is so clear, so evident. (18 September 1992)

The metaphors visually reinforce one teaching that has been on my mind a lot since that day: the importance of beginning the learning with the "core" of knowledge and starting from the inside before going to the surface, the outside. Ellen said:

They said you learn the base, the very basic, the inside, the stem, and the core. It sort of sounds like it when you translate it, the core of what you are learning and then expand out. The teacher will already know that – it is like a big tree, never mind the apples or if it's flowers, we're going to learn inside first and then out, they said. Never from outside first. (White and Archibald 1992, 154)

Ellen's ancestors also said that it is important to take time to sit, think about, and feel what we have learned. My challenge, I realized, was to find this "core" for storywork. Until my encounter with Ellen I had thought more about uncovering the layers of meaning of story – going from the outside surface to the depths. Now, I had to totally rethink this approach and once more go to the unknown to find this particular bone needle.

I visited Ellen a second time, on 11 November 1992, to go over the written transcript for editing purposes. We both had read the transcript individually before meeting; I had mailed her a copy. During my September visit we had agreed to go over it together at our next meeting in order to take out or add information as necessary. I had suggested this process in response to Ellen's question about how I was going to use her talk and about what was going to be put into print. We began to work shortly after I arrived. My journal entry reads:

> Ellen is so good to work with. She knows what words and information that she wants kept in, what might be inappropriate for the readers, and what is culturally inappropriate for this article (i.e., particular healing and spiritual practices). (11 November 1992)

I had not realized that during our initial session Ellen was thinking entirely in Hel'q'emi'nem first about the teachings and knowledge acquired from her ancestors and then translating, or as she says, "looking for the closest English word" to describe what she meant. She had said a few words in Hel'q'emi'nem during the first talk. In this session she shared more Hel'q'emi'nem and talked about the difficulty of finding the right English words to convey her meaning. I felt at a disadvantage because I have only a rudimentary understanding of the Halq'emeylem language, of which Hel'q'emi'nem is one dialect. I noted that I should further examine the problems related to language differences, especially changes of word/concept meaning in translation, with Ellen and other storytellers who are fluent in an Aboriginal language.

This experience with Ellen made me realize some of the complexities of co-operative research work with Elders, such as: (1) needing lots of time to record, listen to, and then transcribe the talk verbatim; (2) examining together the correctness of the English words, which will become the public cultural record for future generations; and (3) ensuring that both co-operating research partners are satisfied with the article before it is printed. The September visit was about four hours long. It took at minimum forty hours to do the transcription and then check back with the audiotape to ensure accuracy of pauses/silences, voice inflection, names, and so on, which I did myself rather than have someone else do it.

Our November visit was also about four hours long. Ellen was directive in identifying sections that were to be deleted. She was thinking foremost about the reader, who might not understand the spiritual ways, and said that if we were to keep these parts, we would have to add more background information, which would then change the intent of her "talk." She also noted that some of the knowledge was not for public use. Ellen took the lead at the beginning of the transcription work, deciding what words and sections were to be kept and what was to be left out, rather than having me first suggest and her agree. I gave her feedback on her directives, and by the end of the transcription our process was similar to that described by Walter Lightning (1992) as "mutual thinking": when we came to certain parts, we simultaneously identified them. I think that our process of getting to know one another, sharing the same cultural traditions, and establishing a consensual working approach led to mutual thinking. Out of the complexities, I gained an appreciation for four principles: (1) respecting each other and the cultural knowledge; (2) responsibly carrying out the roles of teacher and learner (a serious approach to the work and being mindful of what readers/other learners can comprehend); (3) practising reciprocity so that we each gave to the other, thereby continuing the cycle of knowledge from generation to generation; and (4) revering spiritual knowledge and one's spiritual being.

During the *CJNE* sessions with Ellen, I wanted to ask her whether she would agree to work with me on my storywork research. However, I resisted because I wanted her to get to know me better and to see how I would work with her stories and words on the *CJNE* article. More important, I wanted her to trust my motives for and methods of story research. Since September 1992 Ellen has also been involved in two other First Nations curriculum projects with me, both of which use storytelling. We know each other very well, and there is a special connection between us.

I also feel close to Ellen because she is a Coast Salish woman, and I wonder whether the kinds of stories that First Nations women tell are different from stories told by First Nations men. Another storyteller, Louise Profit-Leblanc, of the Yukon Tutchone Nation, introduced this notion: "Women speak to the moral and spiritual fibre, and men speak about the laws of the land" (personal communication and fieldnote, 7 March 1993). So if I am to honour/respect cultural protocol, should I work mainly with First Nations women? Or should I trust that I am being directed to work with whomever I need to or am ready to work with, in a manner similar to that experienced by Maria Campbell? Another question to ponder.

When I was writing my response to Ellen's talk for the *CJNE* article, I felt a strong resistance. This resistance to writing has been so prevalent in my academic work for so long that it has become like a critical friend, one whose positive and negative attributes I have come to know and like. A critical friend also makes me question and reflect while nudging me to move forward. The resistance continues because I do not want to engage in the disrespectful actions of academic outsiders by becoming too explicit and directive in the learning and writing process. From my Stó:lō teachings and from other Indigenous ways, I have learned that in the oral tradition the listener/learner is challenged to make meaning and gain understanding from the storyteller/teacher's words and stories, which is an empowering process. I recall Vincent Stogan's teaching about giving small amounts of information so that the learner keeps coming back to the teacher for more.

From 1992 to 1995 Ellen White and I continued our friendship and worked together on a new curriculum project for kindergarten to Grade 7, First Nations Journeys of Justice, which was sponsored by the Law Courts Education Society of British Columbia. During the curriculum work Ellen became the project Elder with whom the curriculum staff and I consulted. She also participated in the Advisory Committee meetings, shared two stories that created a firm foundation on which to build understanding of working with stories, and was a participant in a teachers' storytelling video. The First Nations Journeys of Justice project, discussed in detail in a later chapter, is a story-based curriculum. Ellen also continued to be one of the Elders-In-Residence with the First Nations House of Learning youth programs, living on campus each summer for a two-week period and participating in the program. During the curriculum project and the youth program, Ellen and I had time to visit and also to talk about storywork. Some of these discussions were tape-recorded or video-recorded because they were for the curriculum project. Ellen agreed to participate in these recorded sessions, and we also agreed that she would maintain copyright of her stories.

I did not ask Ellen to directly participate in my research until the summer of 1995. I was finally ready and culturally "worthy." I was also ready to share with and "give back" to Ellen what I had learned from her – thereby practising the principle of reciprocity. Turning to tradition helped me. I remember the words of Gail High Pine in her article "The Great Spirit in the modern world," where she speaks about the concept of tradition and preservation: "It is not important to preserve our traditions, it is important to allow our traditions to preserve us" (quoted in Hampton 1995, 22). When I let the tradition of cultural reciprocity help me, I was able to let go of those earlier anxious feelings, and I was ready to be guided by respect in order to share knowledge with others who may benefit from this sharing. This readiness is similar to the Elders' desire to pass on their knowledge to others, especially the children and future generations. The teachings that I learned from Kwulasulwut, Ellen White, guided me through the rest of the story-research process and helped me to appreciate the power of stories. In later chapters I will share more of my learning from Kwulasulwut. I was ready to go to my Stó:lō Elder teachers to learn about the storytelling process and to learn more about storywork for educational purposes.

CHAPTER THREE

Learning about Storywork
from Stó:lō Elders

The Coqualeetza Cultural Centre, located at Sardis, British Columbia, provides culturally oriented services and programs to the Stó:lō, to other Aboriginal people, and to non-Aboriginals, particularly teachers. It is one of the many units – which include health, education, social services, treaty negotiations, and political decision making – that form the Stó:lō Nation offices. There is another Elders' group that forms part of the governance of the Stó:lō Nation. In order to distinguish the two Elders' groups, the one associated with the Coqualeetza Cultural Centre is referred to as the "Coqualeetza Elders." These Elders meet regularly to document cultural knowledge and the Halq'emeylem language, to discuss any matter brought before them, and to give cultural counsel to elected chiefs, educators, and students.

The centre began in 1973, at a time when Aboriginal peoples across Canada were engaged in a cultural resurgence movement. This cultural movement was one response to a renewed threat of assimilation of First Nations peoples based on a proposed federal government policy, the White Paper, which intended to obliterate any rights that Indian people had to self-determination (Battiste and Barman 1995). In 1974 I was teaching in the Chilliwack School District. Previously, I had been away from home for six years, going to university, then teaching for two years in North Vancouver. At home, in Chilliwack, I participated in the Halq'emeylem language classes and cultural programs such as cedar-root basket making and hide tanning. I enjoyed these activities because I got to know the Elders and other community people who were teaching and taking the courses and because I learned more about the Stó:lō territory and cultural ways.

Seeking Their Permission and Guidance

The Coqualeetza Elders' Group began in 1970. They would meet at each other's homes to document and tape-record the Halq'emeylem language and their cultural knowledge through storytelling and talk. As the group expanded, it changed its meeting place to the new Coqualeetza Cultural Centre, to what the Stó:lō people call the Big House, a large heritage-like home, which had been the doctor's residence when the Coqualeetza Complex was used as a hospital and tuberculosis sanatorium for First Nations people throughout British Columbia.[1] The first time I walked into this Big House I wondered what the lives of the doctors were like who lived in this huge house over the years, while most Native people lived in crowded, much smaller, poorly constructed, modest homes.

By 1973 the Stó:lō people were using this Big House and had made it "home" to many who came to learn and to share knowledge and friendship. Some of the Elders cooked food for lunch; then after lunch they sat and talked about the cultural ways, recorded the language, and gave advice to the staff about programs. Usually, there were at least thirty. There was always lots of teasing, laughter, and serious talk in both English and Halq'emeylem. From 1975 to 1985 I either worked at Coqualeetza or participated in various courses and committee work. My most memorable learning experiences are from the times I spent with the Elders and other Stó:lō people through the Coqualeetza Cultural Centre's activities.

In 1985 I moved away from home and went back to Vancouver to work as supervisor of the Native Indian Teacher Education Program (NITEP) at the University of British Columbia. The NITEP is a bachelor of education degree program that prepares people of Aboriginal ancestry to be effective teachers. Since moving away, I have continued to assist the Coqualeetza staff with the Stó:lō Sitel curriculum work when requested and have occasionally visited the Elders' Group. Since the Elders' Group started, many have passed on to the Spirit World, leaving a small core who are either fluent Halq'emeylem speakers or knowledgeable about cultural traditions. The Elders' meetings are mainly conducted in English, which shows that the Halq'emeylem language has lost its functional use among our people.[2] Some new Elders have joined the group. They either have moved back to Stó:lō country, have been asked to join the group, or have volunteered themselves. Fortunately, I still know many of the current members of the Elders' Group.

On 19 November 1992 I met with the Elders' Council to ask for its approval and assistance with my storywork research. Approximately seven Elders are appointed to the council as representatives of the Coqualeetza Elders. They make decisions, develop policies, and provide guidance to the offices of the Stó:lō Nation upon request. Council decisions and business matters are always discussed at the weekly meetings of all Elders. I felt that this approval process was important because I am part of the Elders' family and have a responsibility to them to respect their role and authority as teachers. It is respect and caring that guides my feelings and actions, not an obligatory sense of duty. The Elders said that they were glad to see me and noted that I had been away for a long time (fieldnote, 19 November 1992). The family-like relationship that I share with the Elders was affirmed when, at one of the larger meetings, where all Elders and interested persons gather, one Elder said that I was "the Elders' granddaughter" (fieldnote, 18 January 1995).

On 19 November we met at the Big House, sat around a few tables, were served tea and coffee by the Stó:lō Sitel staff, and talked while waiting to begin the meeting. After the prayer, I told them the purpose of my research, and I asked them to be my guides. They were very encouraging, readily agreed to help me, and said that they were glad to see me doing this type of work. My journal entry reads:

> I recall the good warm feelings of being loved and respected by the Elders' Council that day. Going home.
>
> They liked my work and said it was important to do; so many Elders have left us. We talked about the importance of stories for teaching and how they help us to live right – to be good human beings. Such a relief not to be doing this important work alone, but to have guides. (23 November 1992)

During the session we reminisced about some of the memorable storytellers. The people they talked about seemed to meet two definite conditions of good storytelling: (1) people could listen to them for a long, long time, without getting bored, and (2) their stories were remembered.

The council members, with the assistance of the Coqualeetza Cultural Centre's staff, agreed to meet with me on a regular basis and also agreed to ask certain people to join us. They wanted each meeting tape-recorded so that the knowledge embedded in their words would "never be lost." This group was now accustomed to tape-recording what they said at group gatherings and trusted the technology to work. I discussed the possibility of publishing a book based on their discussions and using the royalties for whatever purpose they chose. They suggested either an Elders' fund or a student scholarship fund. We did not spend much time discussing this topic.

Another question that I asked was about protocol: "how do I approach people with whom I would like to talk?" Their reply: "go ask them." They say that being Elders, they have time to do this kind of work and are waiting to be asked. They suggested that one of them could help by going with me to see people whom I didn't know. Their response seems so simple, yet for any researcher, me included, getting this kind of co-operation and support is not an easy matter. I had established a strong familial bond with the Elders over many years and also had the support of the Coqualeetza staff, who liaise with the Elders, who help with the research process by arranging Elders' transportation to the meetings and by providing the meeting space and food, and who are research partici-pants. My research would not have been possible without the assistance of the Coqualeetza staff and if I had not had a personal history with the Elders.

Talking around the Circle

I had four other follow-up meetings with seven to fifteen people at each session; about one-third of the group were men, which is representative of the gender mix of the Elders' Group. Those who regularly attended the meetings included Mary Lou Andrew, Pat Campo, Wilfred Charlie, Amelia Douglas, Jim Fraser, Frank Gardner, Roseline George, Tillie Guiterrez, Ann Lindley, Frank Malloway, Elizabeth Phillips, Roy Point, and Mary Uslick. Sometimes younger Stó:lō community members at-tended the sessions. The Stó:lō Sitel staff looked after the logistical ar-rangements. We usually began the meetings at 10:00 a.m., talked until noon, and continued during lunch. The Elders were taken home by 1:30 p.m. Our meetings were held either in the Big House or in what used to be called the Nurses' Residence, which, at the time of the talks housed the Stó:lō Nation education offices. The following fieldnote de-scribes the physical context of the Nurses' Residence meeting place:

I'm back in this two-storey brick building at the Coqualeetza Complex. Coqualeetza's history: a traditional gathering place where tribes met and women washed clothes and blankets in the nearby stream. (Part of the meaning of Coqualeetza is a gathering place, a cleansing place where blankets were washed. This is still a gathering place where the people talk and do cleansing metaphorically.) It was a residential school, then a hospital, an army residence, and now a cultural centre and houses various Stó:lō Nation offices.

We're meeting in what is now called the Boardroom. Over the years, the Elders' meetings have been held in this room. Sometimes the meetings were shifted to different buildings, but they eventually came back here. There used to be couches is this room; now there are only tables and chairs. There used to be an atmosphere of some informality and comfort; now it seems formal and colder. We rearrange a few tables and chairs into a smaller rectangular space. During the session, many of the speakers refer to us as being in "this circle here." Even though we are not physically in a circle, the teachings and feelings make us talk like we are. (6 December 1992)

The reference in my fieldnote to being in a circle symbolizes the respect that people have for each other and for the purpose of the work that they do when they come together as an Elders' group. Everyone in the circle is treated equally. Not everyone agrees with each other, but everyone agrees that anyone who wants to speak should be given the opportunity. A speaker talks without verbal interruption until she/he is finished. Each person who sits with the Elders in this circle of learning assumes a responsibility to either listen, to share, to teach, or to learn.

During our sessions the Elders and other participants answer my questions with life-experience stories, and they tell traditional stories as well. They often take turns responding when I ask a question and ensure that everyone gets a chance to speak. If a person does not choose to speak, then her/his decision is respected. They respond to each other by asking questions or by teasing each other: once in a while there are tense moments when someone talks too much or not loud enough to be heard. Whenever someone talks too long, others either give the person a stern "look" or avoid eye contact with her/him. If someone does not talk loud enough, they ask her/him to speak up. The people who are here have sat with each other through countless hours of meetings, so they know each other well. They are like an extended family. They show agreement by saying, "yes, that's true, what you say, I remember," and they continue with a supporting type of story. They also prod each other to speak more at times. When they disagree, they don't openly voice it but show difference by introducing a different type of story or by saying, "well, in my family, this is what I heard." When they feel that they are getting "off topic" they say something like: "But that's beside the point; right now we're trying to help Jo-ann."

Our first session focused on the training of speakers, criteria for determining a good storyteller, and issues of respect or lack of respectful practices toward either the speaker or the cultural context for the oral traditions. The second meeting began with my questions about storytelling for children: When were children told stories? What kinds of stories? How did one know when to tell a particular kind of story? Each person began to speak about her/his personal experiences. But one man's life-experience story emphasized the spiritual/sacred, which he said he normally didn't talk about. One of the Stó:lō cultural rules regarding spiritual/sacred experiences is not to talk about them. When he was talking I did not write anything down, but the tape-recorder was on. Others began to tell similar kinds of stories. As they finished their stories, each one said with strong conviction, "It is true!" Afterward, I wondered why they told such stories when they shouldn't have. When I got home I checked the cassette tape and found that the discussion had not been recorded. I ponder the meaning of this apparent coincidence. At the beginning of the third session, I felt embarrassed telling the group that the tape recorder had not worked. I mentioned that perhaps we were not supposed to have taped the talk because of what was said about the spiritual. We got into a discussion about the dilemma of following a cultural rule that could result in important knowledge becoming extinct because it is not passed onto someone else. We talked about the need to teach the younger generation this type of Stó:lō knowledge and the traditional stories. Implied here is the ability to understand the "teachings" (values, beliefs, lessons, and symbolism) of the stories. At the end of this meeting, the Elders said that they did not have any more to say about storytelling. I made a commitment to take what they had said, speak to others, write down what I had learned, and come back to share this learning with them.

Two years later, I came back with a draft of a chapter to verify with the Elders' Council. We started to meet again in December 1995. The verification process continued until December 1996. I met with individuals, gave copies of drafted chapters to Coqualeetza staff, and met with the

Elders' Council.[3] Two new female council members joined in the talks. I also interviewed two Coqualeetza staff members, Shirley Leon, the manager, and Peter Lindley, the curriculum co-ordinator. The quotations used from the 1992-94 sessions were approved by the appropriate individuals. In the verification process, I started with a question that I had asked in the first session: What makes a good storyteller?

What Makes a Good Storyteller?

Two memorable storytellers who have gone to the Spirit World, Dolly Felix and Ed Leon, were talked about when I asked who were/are good storytellers and what made/makes them good. As they were identified, I could visualize both telling their stories at various gatherings almost fifteen years earlier. Each had a way of bringing out the humour in the story, and each had an animated manner: Ed with actions, Dolly with her voice. She was blind and used a wheelchair. The gifted storytellers took on the persona of the characters in their stories.

> The greatest storyteller was Ed Leon. He could make any little story funny. Just the way he tells it, the expressions he uses, the actions. It wasn't just using your mouth, it was using your hands, using your body, to get the story out. Ed was the greatest storyteller I know. (Frank Malloway, transcript, 3 December 1992)

Shirley Leon tells of a storytelling incident in which Dolly Felix captured the attention of seventy-five kindergarten children:

> [At] one of the first Chehalis Pioneer Day sessions that we participated in, Dolly was going to do the storytelling, and somehow the scheduling got mixed up and we ended up with seventy-five kindergarten children. We were wondering, "how are we going to pull this off?" There's no way we could get seventy-five kids to sit still for a story with Dolly because she really elaborates. But I guess ... she just had that knack. I think a storyteller's effective if you believe in what you're saying. When she was telling the Th'oxwiya story, it just became a part of her ... There wasn't a pin that could have dropped, unheard, in that hall during the storytelling because she got totally involved with the story. And for years after, the teachers commented, what a miracle that was that she was able to capture their attention. I just think when people are gifted with storytelling, the stories become so much a part of their character

and that's what really captures peoples' attention. (Transcript, 5 December 1995)

Ed and Dolly are gone, but their stories and story spirit live on in the memories of people who saw and heard them. Some of their stories live (but not as strongly) on the printed pages of storybooks and on cassette tapes. Fortunately, we have some Elders and younger people who are trying to keep storytelling alive today.

Becoming Storytellers: The Role of Mentors and Teachers

Two Coqualeetza Elders, Tillie Guiterrez and Ann Lindley, are storytellers called upon to tell stories in classrooms, and they also tell stories at meetings and cultural gatherings. Both were told stories by mentors, who were their relatives, when they were young children. Tillie's grandfather and someone else's grandfather brought her to a place with special "rocks" and began to teach her stories about place names and spiritual matters. When Tillie talks about what is important to her as a storyteller, the influence of her spiritual teachings stands out: "I start with the stories from way back. I always start when X̱á:ls came. I never actually stand up there by myself. I have to have him with me in order to be able to stand in front of people" (transcript, 3 December 1992). X̱á:ls is the Stó:lō transformer figure, or Creator, who, in our traditional stories, helps bring order to a chaotic world. Sometimes X̱á:ls changes people to elements of the environment, not as punishment but as a symbol of the goodness that the individual has performed. X̱á:ls's transformations remind us about the close connections that humans have to nature.[4] Ann's aunt told her niece stories when she was a child, often before meal times "when there was time to kill" (fieldnote, 14 January 1993).

From the accounts of Simon Baker, Vincent Stogan, and the Coqualeetza Elders, it seems that Elders who now are the experts of the oral traditions had teachers in their childhood, often their relatives, who told them stories and prepared them to become storytellers and speechmakers. However, they did not assume these roles until later in life. Their "training" began as a child, and during their early to middle adult years they continued to work, raise children, and be a marriage partner and community worker. Often, the time to engage in the oral traditions was limited because of these factors. In their later adult years, the responsibility to teach the cultural ways through the oral traditions became theirs. Some, like Simon Baker and Vincent and Edna Stogan, realized that their Elders were passing away and that they were going to be the next Elders, so they assumed this role. Others were suddenly pushed into the role, like Ann Lindley, who told of her realization of her storytelling "gift" and purpose in life. My fieldnotes describe what occurred:

> Each one of us was put here for something. Wilfred Charlie, who was co-ordinating the Elders' Group, asked her and the late Jean Silver if they wanted to take a drive on this nice sunny day. They ended up in the Langley area. Wilfred told them that a "white lady" was wanting them to tell stories in the school. He said that he would sit with them. So they were "put on the spot." It was at this point that Anne started to tell stories with Jean. She said that she didn't know that she had these stories in her memory until this time: stories told to her by her aunt. During her adult years she was too busy raising children and did not remember the stories. So this was how her purpose and gift came to her.[5] (Fieldnotes, 14 January 1993 and 8 January 1996)

Wilfred Charlie, who worked as the Elders' co-ordinator, reinforces the responsibility of teaching the oral tradition and culture to young children. He also uses his own personal life experience to show that he had to learn how to work with and talk with Elders in his later adult years. Many Stó:lō people have not had the opportunity to learn directly from Elders because the traditional intergenerational learning process was severed for many years when institutional schooling, the residential-school era, was forced upon First Nations. It is my generation that has lost many of the cultural ways, and we need to work vigilantly to regain them. My child's generation at least has more First Nations curricula and cultural-education programs because of the efforts of the Elders about whom I write. Some of these Elders are gaining their rightful place as cultural teachers as they tell stories to students in band and public schools, to postsecondary students, and to adults who ask. Wilfred Charlie explains how he got involved:

> We were talking about the speakers ... you got to teach them when they're young, explain your subject or story or whatever you're going to talk about. Skulkale [my reserve], got a little grant for culture [in 1969]. I had to learn how to speak to the Elders, to learn how to get back some of our culture.

Then the centre come in: Coqualeetza. I got involved. I was one of the first to be involved with the Elders ... Many tapes of the old people, that never went to school [were recorded with them speaking Halq'e-meylem and telling stories] ... culture wasn't lost. That's where we got a lot of our information from them ... people like Mary Peters, she knew everything.

I am still learning how to speak to the Elders. All them years, ... I had to get out and learn. It's not an easy job. You have to know how to get up and speak to people. They only speak on one subject ... that's a very important thing in the Stó:lō, we need public speakers, we are short of speakers. That's a little about my background. I try to teach my own children ... you have to keep after them ... I'm seventy-six and I've been studying since 1964, that's where my strength comes from ... Your turn Frank [the group members tease one another and laugh]. (Transcript, 3 December 1992)

During the meetings, there was much laughter. Humour through teasing, joking, and telling funny stories is a very important cultural interaction. Humour indicates that the group is comfortable with and open to each other – and to the researcher. If humour is absent from a research session, then one could question the validity of the information shared because the Elders may not have felt comfortable and therefore may not have given sufficient or adequate information. Above, I quoted Frank Malloway's comment that one of the best Stó:lō storytellers was Ed Leon, who made his life-experience stories very funny. I remember hearing Ed tell these stories, and even though they may have had a serious incident in them, he was able to make people laugh. I believe that humour has a healing aspect for both the storyteller and the listener in that those who have lived through very difficult circumstances and who can share some humorous aspect of the experience have achieved some emotional or spiritual healing and resilience. Those who hear and appreciate the humour are given hope for healing if they need it.

Some of the intergenerational responsibility of teaching cultural knowledge has been reclaimed by Elders who teach young people the oral tradition. Each one has a different approach, but the important point is that they too learned storytelling from a teacher. Perhaps more individual mentoring and teaching is needed to "train" more people to become storytellers:

So with this little bit of knowledge that we have, like Frank is trying to hand it down to the young ones in the longhouse, Wilfred's trying to hand his down, this is good. I like to tell stories because there's morals in those stories that give me help. Even if you don't know it all, you still tell it because of the moral. The skunk story that I tell has morals in it. That was told to me over and over, night after night, you know, it was told to me so many times it just stuck in there, I never had to write it down. The morals of that story are not to brag, or show off. (Tillie Guiterrez, transcript, 3 December 1992)

Not everyone who knows stories and knows the oral traditions becomes a storyteller. However, those who have been given the "gift" for the oral traditions were mentored or taught by someone to fulfil this role. It is critical that Stó:lō Elders continue to mentor and teach some of the younger generation storytelling techniques/skills.

Training for Oratory[6]

The responses to the question of how one becomes a good storyteller, besides the individual mentoring process, focused on some basic oratory skills and training, such as speaking in a loud but not forceful voice, standing up when speaking, and stopping if needless repetition occurs. These skills were developed at the same time as one was learning about the substantive content of stories and speeches. The voice training of longhouse speakers occurred in nature, not in the longhouse, as Frank Malloway recounts:

One of the things about voice training I was told, the old people used to take the young men [who were to be the Spokesmen] down to small creeks, you know. The teacher would go on one side and the one in training on the other side and sit and talk to them. And you'd have to talk loud enough for him to hear. Then they'd go to a bigger river. "You talk to me, don't you scream at me, talk to me." That's how they did the training, you had to speak loud enough so that the old man could hear him. It was sort of a gradual thing. That was one of the ways that they used to train people. (Transcript, 3 December 1992)

At one time, people lived in the longhouses, so these dwellings would not have been an appropriate place for this type of learning. The Spokesman[7] was taught the stories, cultural principles, and practices because he had to know all these to carry out his job. Because the significant events went on for hours, sometimes days, the Spokesman's voice had to last, even though there was more than one Spokesman. Chief Richard Malloway, a respected leader and speaker, warned his son Frank about the needless use of repetition during one's talk:

> When I first started speaking at functions, my father used to coach me. He used to always say: "When you find yourself repeating things, you know it's time to sit down. You don't tell the same thing over and over. People will get tired of listening to you and they'll turn you off. They'll start talking to somebody else." So he says, "as soon as you catch yourself repeating words or phrases, it's time to sit down."[8] (Transcript, 3 December 1992)

Frank mentions how his father, his oratory teacher, also challenged him through competitive means to become a good speaker. This example shows how the teacher challenged the learner in a positive way:

> One of the ways my father taught me to be a good speaker, an interesting speaker, used to challenge me. You know, we were called to witness at a funeral dinner. He'd tell me "you go first," make me speak first, then I'd get up there and talk, walking back to my seat "I can do better than that," he says [laughs]. He'd get up and make a better speech than me. I used to expect this. Next time, he says go up, I'd try and make a better speech, short and sweet. "Oh, I can beat that," he says. Every time he'd get me to speak first. He was always there to challenge, "to do better than your dad. Speak better than your dad." But he was hard to beat ... That was one of his ways to teach me to speak better, to make more interesting speeches. (Transcript, 3 December 1992)

It must be remembered that these basic skills and stories were learned without the use of literacy; therefore, one's memory skills became highly developed. Roy Point puts it this way: "They had memories, miles and miles long with their stories" (transcript, 6 December 1995). Hearing stories over and over again was part of the storyteller's training, which began in her/his childhood and happened in contexts where telling stories seemed a natural part of daily life. This type of story repetition is not the needless repetition mentioned earlier.

Storytelling Contexts: The Longhouse, Land, and Home

The longhouse was the traditional location for telling stories. In the past and today, some of the storytelling training is done on the land or in the home. Each of these contexts is distinct from the other.

Speaking in the Longhouse: "The old school, the old teaching place of the people"

Frank Malloway is an Elder Spokesman called upon to speak at traditional gatherings. His job is to speak for the family hosting the event, talk about traditions, family history, and rules, and ensure that the event's activities are carried out in an organized manner. The oral traditions are the predominant means of communication for all activities that take place in the Stó:lō longhouse, and time is not a driving force: "there is no time set on anything that's taking place" (Frank Malloway, transcript, 3 December). Literacy has no place here.

Our longhouses are sometimes called smokehouses. They are huge cedar-plank buildings, and the largest in the Stó:lō Nation seats several hundred people. Sacred winter ceremonies are practised by many in the smokehouses. Other cultural gatherings and meetings are held in some of the longhouses during the months that the winter ceremonies are not practised. The Stó:lō Nation education office has built a smaller version of a longhouse, which is used only for cultural-education programs.

The Stó:lō longhouse is associated with a strong spiritual practice that encompasses teachings about respect for all beings and living a healthy lifestyle. There are strict cultural protocols and rules about behaviour, whether one is a guest, a hosting family/community, or a speaker. Frank shares his concern about people who have not been taught cultural protocol or the cultural rules for types of talks, and he notes his teaching responsibility toward them. Particular types of speeches and stories have an appropriate structure that is to be followed in the longhouse.

> One of the things that a lot of our people are doing [wrong] in the longhouse, you're called to witness certain work, and when you get up to talk, you only talk about what you're about to witness. You don't go and talk about something else ... That's what a lot of our young people are doing. One of these days I have to take them aside and talk to them. You don't talk about your achievements in life [when you are] called to witness a little job. That's really disrespectful. It's like saying well your

work is not that important. My past life is more important, I'll tell about it. It's a sign of disrespect. But they haven't been taught. (Transcript, 3 December 1992)

Shirley Leon reinforces the notion that the longhouse traditional values teach respectful behaviour toward others, and she attributes the negative influence of mainstream education to those who act disrespectfully:

How are you going to explain the difference in training, how you respect people, that's what it boils down to, you know, the storyteller and listener. I always use the analogy if you look at the smokehouse people, you go into the longhouses, the environment there, the way they talk to each other, greet each other, it is so different than if you go to an education meeting or band or tribal meeting. Look at the environment, how different it is, just those two places ... Scholars will call that different domains. But those people that got training in the longhouse, when they come here, you notice, I'm sure the Elders notice, soon as they walk in they don't wait to be told to help clean or serve the Elders. They'll notice some Elders might have tea. They notice they might need help. They just pitch in and start helping. They don't have to be told. Old Choppy used to always comment on that at the Elders' meeting with visitors. He'd say, "you can sure tell they got good teachings." They'd sit and listen, they'd pitch in and help. They don't get up and walk out when someone is talking. Don't matter if it's not important to them. They're showing respect. It's hard to explain the difference. It's just like some people when they get an education they think they're God, you know, just because they have an education. They have no patience with anybody ... So different backgrounds. (Transcript, 3 December 1992)

The longhouse is a natural cultural context for carrying on the oral traditions. Many Stó:lō do not engage in the winter ceremonial lifestyle and may not have the same opportunity to learn the traditional values and teachings that Frank and Shirley mention, which are an important requirement for learning how to listen to stories and make meaning from them. This particular problem is now being addressed through the introduction of educational programs and storytelling sessions that are held in some of the longhouses during the summer months, which is not contrary to traditional ways. During the verification sessions, some of the Coqualeetza Elders referred to the longhouse as "the old school, the old teaching place of the people."

Telling Stories about and on the Land

Another natural context for learning stories is the land. The term "land" includes the earth and its relation, water. The importance of learning stories from the grandparents about the land, while being on the land, was reinforced for me. Mary Lou Andrew remembers hearing stories when doing chores and walking from place to place:

> Stories were told when children were being taught how to sew, how to do laundry ... in my childhood, my grandmother, my grandfather, always had stories ... [when] walking through the fields or if you went to gather fruit or food, or if you were just going from point A to point B, there was a story to be told about the area [its place name] or [a historical story of] what happened at that place.

Mary Lou also points out that learning through stories has an interrelated aspect:

> Sometimes it took a long time to get there. You got not only history about the place, the land; you were taught [other] lessons ... You got social studies ... sometimes even science was thrown in, when you had to deal with herbs and medicines. You learned the importance of why you do something; like why you walked on a certain part of the pathway, so that you didn't destroy certain plants. (Transcript, 6 December 1995; verification session, 8 October 1996)

Along with the stories, the Elders gave important teachings, such as the protection of plants, through their talks with the children. Place-name stories show that the names not only have meanings but are also associated with practices and values, such as the spiritual connection with a particular mountain. Mary Uslick describes the seamless connection between land and people, which is a critical teaching that Elders want continued:

> When our ancestors talk about our mountains, our rivers, our trees, and our lakes, they got names for all these places ... The names of the mountains and everything was given by our ancestors because it had a meaning, when it [the name] was given, and it should be respected ... That's how they teach the children about it. First of all, they must know the name of that mountain, why the old people call it that. Like Tamahi. We give our offering, we face it, that's where the sun comes

out. These children have to learn to respect these [teachings] and then they will teach their children our stories. They will know the names of our mountains, the rivers ... Those are the kind of stories that the old people tell so the children ... will remember these things, what's going to be their area when they grow up. (Transcript, 6 December 1995)

In these contexts, storytelling was not a public event but was more individualized, emphasizing connections and responsibilities to the land. Again, values and respectful practices were intertwined with identity, places, and place-name stories.

The interrelationship between place, Indigenous identity, and place-based stories has been reinforced by Indigenous scholars such as N. Scott Momaday (1968), Vine Deloria Jr. (1992), and Leslie Marmon Silko (1981) and by non-Indigenous scholars such as Keith Basso (1996) and Julie Cruikshank (1981, 1990, 2005). Leslie Marmon Silko's description of the relationship between Pueblo stories and the land resonates with the Stó:lō Elders' experiences as described by Mary Lou Andrew:

The stories cannot be separated from geographical locations, from actual physical places within the land ... And the stories are so much a part of these places that it is almost impossible for future generations to lose the stories because there are so many imposing geological elements ... you cannot live in the land without asking or looking at or noticing a boulder or rock. And there's always a story. (Silko, quoted in Basso 1996, 64)

Telling Stories in the Home

"[The Elders] started [children] very young towards respect ... [with] the stories of the animals." (Mary Uslick, transcript, 6 December 1995)

Another informal approach to storytelling occurred in the home. Some of the Elders recalled hearing stories from their grandparents before going to sleep at night. It seems that grandparents also had the responsibility to teach young children proper behaviour. Roy Point recalls:

The way our people were taught ... went by our old people ... At bedtime, when the little ones were ready to go to sleep, they had a story for everything that had to be taught to that young one. Usually [the story] came out when something that little one done, that needed to be taught ... for instance, a little boy went into stealing ... then my grandfather ... would have a story for that ... The parents never had too much [to do] with the teachings, they had to ... provide the food. The grandparents provide the teachings. (Transcript, 6 December 1995)

It seems that the grandparents never explicitly linked the story with the name of the grandchild to whom it was directed, but she/he knew what was being implied. These stories were not told during brief episodes in the evenings. As Roy recalls, the stories were told "for a couple to three hours," so children became accustomed to listening to stories for a long time. He also mentions that the grandparents "had memories, miles and miles long with their stories" (transcript, 6 December 1995). These nighttime stories were about animals, and the lessons not only related to behaviour but also taught children the close relationship that Stó:lō people had to animals, as explained by Mary Uslick: "[The Elders] started [children] very young towards respect ... [with] the stories of the animals, they understand ... what they are to us people" (transcript, 6 December 1995).

Language issues surfaced when Jim Fraser said that he could not speak much Halq'emeylem, only "easy words." His grandfather used to tell nighttime stories in Halq'emeylem, and his sister Agnes would translate the stories into English for Jim. Hearing the story in two different languages was confusing at first. But he remembers that the "bad stories" were about Coyote, which fits the Trickster's way of teaching better behaviour and esteemed values. Jim said that the radio "knocked stories from the Elders" (transcript, 9 October 1996). He meant that radio, as a new technology at the time, was another factor that contributed to stopping the practices of storytelling and of using the Halq'emeylem language in the home.

During the verification session of 9 October 1996 the Elders' Council talked more about the differences between the Halq'emeylem language and English. They said that the stories lost their humour and some of their meaning during the translation process. What was funny in Halq'emeylem wasn't funny in English. There are words or concepts in Halq'emeylem that can't be described with English words. Since I am not a Halq'emeylem speaker, I accept what I have heard many Stó:lō Elders say over the years: "It's not funny anymore." But the Elders and others have continued to tell stories in the English language, as it is the predominant language of the Stó:lō people today. Maintaining the humour, integrity, and power of stories is even more difficult, but not impossible, in the English language and in contemporary learning contexts. Learning to listen to stories in a traditional way may help to establish an appreciation for the Stó:lō stories told in English.

But more efforts to learn and to use the Halq'emeylem language need to occur. Ethel Gardner (2002), a Stó:lō scholar, documents the initiatives to revitalize the Halq'emeylem language.

Story Listening

> "We have three ears to listen with, two on the sides of our head and
> one in our heart"

Many of the Elders kept saying that it was and is important to learn how to listen. Roseline George said that one had to "listen, watch, and not talk while the story is told" (transcript, 3 December 1992). Listening requires the concomitant involvement of the auditory and visual senses, the emotions, the mind, and patience. The act of story listening occurs in relation to using our other senses. I have heard Stó:lō and other First Nations storytellers say that we have "three ears to listen with, two on the sides of our head and one in our heart." Bringing heart and mind together for story listening was necessary if one was to make meaning from a story because often one was not explicitly told what the story's meanings were. Linking how we feel to what we know was an important pedagogy.[9] Shirley Leon said, "The old way, you had to really think ... you had to figure it out, they wouldn't give you the answer, you had to figure it out." Ann Lindley responded to Shirley, "Therefore, you had to listen, otherwise you'd miss it" (transcript, 6 December 1995).

Many Indigenous gatherings open with a prayer, song, or ceremony like burning sweetgrass or sage to symbolize cleansing the mind/body/spirit to get ready to listen in the manner described above. Centring, quieting oneself, is another way to get ready for story listening. When people have hand drums they will beat them after some of the speaker's words to show their appreciation for the thought, and some will say, "Ho!" – which means that they are listening. I think that these are examples of how one can take care of the speaker. The speaker/storyteller appreciates these signals of listening. Reciprocally, the storyteller can take care of others by selecting the appropriate story to tell. Sometimes, one's intuitive power helps with the selection.

"Reading the Situation": Story Intuitiveness

In a later chapter I will recount my experience of becoming a story-teller and letting a story-intuitive approach guide the selection of which story is to be told. Peter Lindley, Ann's son, said that his mother does something similar: "That's one thing ... she always says, 'Don't ever tell me what story I'm going to tell them. I'll know when I get there. I read them [the students]. I read that teacher'" (transcript, 5 December 1995). Ann's "reading" of the participants and her intuitive process come from the interaction of the storyteller, the story listeners, and the context that brings everyone together. However, it is the ultimate responsibility of the storyteller to know which story to tell and to know how much to tell or explain about story meaning. Some storytellers say nothing about meaning, while others give an example of a meaning, or a "moral," as some call it. I believe that the need to explicate meaning depends on how good the listeners are at making their own understandings from stories and the ability of the storyteller to determine this. I think back to Vincent Stogan's words about the Elder directing one's learning by knowing how much to teach at each learning session. Peter echoes his mother's teaching, which she learned from another Elder, about the intended effect of this kind of incremental teaching approach: "[Ann] always remembers what Joe Lorenzetto told her, 'Don't tell them every-thing, give them enough to keep them curious all the time'" (transcript, 5 December 1995). This curiosity may make the listener wonder why a particular story was told, or something in the story may leave the lis-tener in a perplexed or unsettled state.

The story "Coyote's Eyes," presented in Chapter 1, seems to end abrupt-ly, without a tidy conclusion, which should make the listener wonder how Coyote will resolve the differences with which he ends up. The value of respect for a sacred kind of knowledge was broken, so perhaps a clue to Coyote's problem is to find out how to respect certain types of Indigen-ous knowledge and to teach/learn it in a culturally appropriate way.

Raising Some Issues

During our sessions, the Elders brought up some other issues related to storytelling that needed resolution. Each of them caused me to ponder.

Breaking Cultural Rules

The dilemma of practising a cultural rule that could result in the loss of important cultural knowledge was brought up by Roy Point in relation to not divulging "secret" and sacred knowledge:

> Some of the things I said weren't supposed to be brought out at all. The old people used to say, "when you see something like that, (like what I told), you're not supposed to tell anyone." How are we going to learn our history, now that it's getting lost, without telling it? We are taught to not let go of any of our own teachings and our own ways, medicines, our own teachings of each tribe, our own secrets. That's the way it was. Now that [knowledge] is being lost. How to keep it alive is a really big question, because so many of our older people are gone, just a handful of us left ... I don't know how we can keep it alive. (Transcript, 28 January 1993).

When Roy speaks of not letting go of, or not sharing, certain knowledge, he means that traditionally one could neither teach nor learn certain things without the cultural authority to do so. To acquire this authority, one first had to complete rigorous training, which involved individualized learning through the oral tradition. This type of knowledge had to be respected because it was associated with some type of power, such as spiritual or healing power. If the knowledge was not used properly and wisely, negative results might occur, and the power contained in the knowledge would not work. Putting any of this knowledge into written form or into another medium was (and still is) considered an extreme violation of this cultural rule. Today, people are asked not to photograph or tape-record the spiritual cultural activities that take place. Roy's concerns that such knowledge is not being passed on to the younger generation and that this knowledge will be lost if the rule is upheld are important ones with which others wrestle. The oral tradition is crucially needed in these circumstances.

Our Elders need to teach younger Stó:lō people sacred knowledge through the oral tradition in order to ensure that the knowledge does not die. If it does, then a critical part of Stó:lō identity will die with it. Perpetuating cultural knowledge while at the same time trying to respect this cultural rule will continue to raise concerns. This question can be a guiding principle: How will the culture and the people be hurt by this action? The important point is that we need to discuss these issues and take responsibility for action.

Reclaiming Responsibility

More Coqualeetza Elders are reclaiming their role of teaching and taking on the responsibility of giving direction to those who work at Coqualeetza and the Stó:lō Nation's offices. The teaching/helping role that Elders had is not forgotten and is being perpetuated by people such as Mary Uslick:

> Storytelling, a long time ago ... when something happened to a family, we used to go and say to the people, go get this Elder. Go get that Elder, [to] teach them. Have them there, it's their guidance. [The Elder] knows what to say to the people ... The way our ancestors taught us ... is very important to remember. And that's what it [oral tradition] is today, to share with the people. What I know better ... that's what I do. (Transcript, 6 December 1995)

The Elders' talk about the loss of some of the traditions contains sentiments of longing for what has been lost, but it also contains thoughts, said with conviction, that they can do something about this concern. They are not completely powerless. Pat Campo said: "We've allowed it [loss of cultural ways] to happen to us, and it's got to stop, it's got to go back to the old ways because the old way was good" (transcript, 6 December 1995). One example of how the "old way" can continue that resonates with tradition is given by Mary Uslick, who conducts circle meetings at various communities within the Stó:lō Nation. Children and adults attend. She uses stories, songs, and talk in the circle. At one of the earlier meetings, Roseline George suggested a solution to Roy Point's question of how to keep Indigenous knowledge alive: "We need to practice it [Indigenous knowledge and the oral tradition] with the little ones to keep it alive" (transcript, 28 January 1993). Mary uses the oral tradition to teach not only the young ones but also the adults, who may become the next storytellers.

During these meetings, it became evident to me, and I think to the group, that we do not have too many storytellers left. However, we are fortunate to still have some active storytellers who go to the schools to tell stories and who continue to tell stories at cultural events. The school as a place for storytelling is not a natural context, as described earlier by the Elders. But it is a place that our children attend. The Elders and the Stó:lō educators continue to hope that the school can be a place where children can hear and learn from stories; this is why they continue to go there to tell stories when they are asked. One suggestion that came up during these meetings is that we start training new storytellers to meet the increasing demand for storytelling in educational contexts and to ensure a continuation of our oral tradition.

Training New Storytellers

The process of mentoring younger family members and teaching them the oral traditions was practised with our Elders, who learned from their ancestors; now the Elder generation is continuing this teaching tradition. Dolly Felix's granddaughter Gwen Point teaches by telling Dolly's stories; Roy Point's son Steven carries on the family's stories and takes on the Spokesman's role; Ann Lindley's son Peter is learning to tell stories by observing his mother and working on cultural-education programs for Coqualeetza; and Frank Malloway is mentoring many young people who are part of the longhouse family. The important point is that whoever is learning the oral tradition has mentors and teachers, and a familial relationship is established. The new storytellers are learning the oral tradition within social/cultural/educational situations – learning by practising it. They are learning mainly through oral teachings, not from textbooks. I do not mean to imply that literacy has no place in learning to be a storyteller. Gwen and Steven Point, Peter Lindley, the Elder storytellers, and I too may read books to learn what others say about the oral traditions and find stories to use that have been put into textual form. However, the foundation for learning to tell stories must be passed on from personal interaction with a storyteller. I believe that it is the good storytellers who will contribute the most to keeping the stories alive.

Keeping the Stories Alive

Shirley and Peter recollect an occasion when the Elders collectively remembered one of the stories, "The Mischievous Cubs," that was used in the Stó:lō Sitel curriculum. This story had not been told for a long time but was buried in people's memories. Bringing back stories that have been "put to sleep in people's memories," as the Elders say, is work that is taken seriously, takes time, and is not without disagreements:

> No one had the whole story. Eventually, they got the whole story pieced together, but it went through a ... transition of convincing each other that their particular part of the memory was valid. It didn't matter if they didn't know all of it. Once they put it all together it became a whole story ... It was incredible listening to the arguments and [talk

about] how long it has been handed down. Teresa Michel was the one that started it ... It was about a year, illustrating and working on it ... When it was finished another piece of [the story] came back at one of our first gatherings with students. [Teresa] said, "Oh, I remember another chapter." (Shirley Leon, transcript, 5 December 1995)

Reawakening the memories that hold some of the forgotten stories and reawakening the storytelling ability of the Elders and other Stó:lō people who have grown up with the oral traditions are necessary if the stories and the ability to make story meaning are to stay alive, especially in a world dominated by literacy and other forms of media such as television, video, and digital technology. Even though the latter may allow for the use of visual images and the sounds of the storyteller, the same questions that confront the relationship between orality and literacy apply: How can the story be portrayed so that its power to make one think, feel, and reflect on one's actions is not lost? Can the cultural context be sufficiently developed so that the listener/viewer can make story meaning?

Roy Point said, "There's a story for every stage of life" (transcript, 6 December 1995). We need to get back all these stories and learn how to use them in educational and community contexts. The Coqualeetza Cultural Centre and the Elders have concentrated on the children's stories, some place-name stories, and some family-history stories. The children's stories could be used at any age level, but more attention could be given to stories oriented to adults, particularly parents and leaders.

As I reflect on my meetings with the Elders, many years later, I feel positive about the story-research process that we shared because it exemplifies what research should do: enable people to sit together and talk meaningfully about how their Indigenous knowledge could be effectively used for education and for living a good life and to think about possibilities for overcoming problems experienced in their communities. During the sessions we realized that many of the Stó:lō traditional storytelling practices have been lost; however, we also acknowledged that some of the oral traditions are still practised in contexts like the longhouse and that some of the stories have been transformed for use in educational curricula. We realized that there are a handful of Elder storytellers who are teaching with stories and teaching some of the younger generation the techniques of the oral traditions. I also realized that others – parents, community members, tribal-council/cultural workers, educators, and students – who could help revitalize the oral traditions needed to sit with us in the Elders' story circle. Hearing what the Elders said during our talks helped me to continue with the purpose that I was given by those who spoke to me in my dream. The Elders' shared stories, traditional knowledge, and guidance reinforced the notion of power that stories once had and could still have. I was ready to begin using storywork in educational contexts.

CHAPTER FOUR

The Power of Stories to Educate the Heart

Each Aboriginal nation has particular traditions, protocols, and rules concerning stories and the way that stories are to be told for teaching and learning purposes. The types of stories can vary from the sacred to the historical, from cultural traditions to personal life experiences and testimonials. Some stories are just for fun, while others have powerful "teachings." Some stories may be "owned," those that are the responsibility of individuals, clans, or families; some belong to the "public domain," being available for anyone to tell. Some stories can be told only at certain times of the year.

In addition to knowing the cultural protocols and rules pertaining to the telling of stories, one must know how to make meaning with stories. It is important to appreciate the diversity among Indigenous cultures and to recognize that there are different story genres, purposes, protocols, and ways to make story meaning. Wapaskwan, who is Walter Lightning's mentor, shared some characteristics of Aboriginal stories and some guiding principles for reading, listening to, and interpreting them:

> The way to interpret those stories has never been clear to the literate, academic community until recently. The stories are not just "texts," or narratives that deal with sequences of events in a linear progression of events.
>
> There are several classes of stories. For example, there are "sacred" stories as opposed to "historical

stories," and traditionally it has taken 40 years or so of apprenticeship for an individual to work to gain the authority to tell the sacred class of story. That length of time is not required just to learn the texts of the stories, nor how to perform them. It takes that long to acquire the principles for interpretation of the stories.

There is a "surface" story: the text, and the things one has to know about the performance of it for others. The stories are metaphoric, but there are several levels of metaphor involved. The text, combined with the performance, contains a "key" or a "clue" to unlock the metaphor. When a hearer has that story, and knows the narrative sequence of it, there is another story contained within that story, like a completely different embedded or implicit text.

The trick is this: that the implicit or embedded text, itself, contains clues, directions – better yet, specifications – for the interpretation of an implicit text embedded in it ... A hearer isn't meant to understand the story at all levels, immediately. It is as if it unfolds. (Wapaskwan, quoted in Lightning 1992, 229-30)

The Stó:lō categorize oral narratives into sxwoxwiyam and squelqwel. Sxwoxwiyam are "myth-like stories set in the distant past." They usually explain how things came to be and how to "make things right for the present generation" (Carlson 1997, 2). Squelqwel are "true stories or news" describing "experiences in peoples' lives" (182). In Stó:lō and Coast Salish cultures the power of storywork to make meaning derives from a synergy between the story, the context in which the story is used, the way that the story is told, and how one listens to the story. The storywork principles of interrelatedness and synergy are woven into this chapter.

Here, the focus is on my experiential story about learning to become a beginning storyteller, which, I have come to realize, began long before I undertook my own storywork research with Elders. Much earlier I was already being taught the significance of stories as a source of education and as a means to achieve emotional wellness.

Becoming a Storyteller

We come from a tradition of storytelling, and as storytellers we have a responsibility to be honest, to transmit our understanding of the world to other people ... In this process, there is something more than information being transmitted: there's energy, there's strength being transmitted from the storyteller to the listener and that is what's important in teaching young people about their identity. (Cuthand 1989, 54)

I have felt the story energy and strength of which Beth Cuthand speaks. This energy is a source of power that feeds and revitalizes mind, heart, body, and spirit in a holistic manner. The strength of stories challenges me to think, to examine my emotional reactions in relation to plot and characters, to question and reflect on my behaviours and future actions, and to appreciate a story's connections to my spiritual nature.

Learning to Make Meaning from Stories

My appreciation for the cultural values of respect, responsibility, reciprocity, and reverence embedded in Indigenous stories did not occur until I let the Elders' teachings about storywork guide me. I did not intentionally set out to become a storyteller, but I did set out to learn more about the nature of Indigenous stories and how they could be used to produce quality education. I am a beginning storyteller who is gaining understandings about the significant role that stories can play in teaching, learning, and healing. My experiential story is told to exemplify the cultural values and to introduce some issues related to story memory, letting Elders guide a learning process, learning patience, and appreciating silence. The power of a story is shown through stories about a story.[1]

My memories of encountering First Nations stories in school curricula go back to my teaching experiences in elementary schools from 1972 to 1979. I also have faint memories of learning about a few Indian legends through the subjects of reading and social studies during my elementary and high school years. These memories are ones that I have tried to forget or to ignore because I felt humiliation and emotional pain over the way that the Indian cultures and peoples were represented and studied. Indian stories and by implication Indian cultures and peoples were portrayed as simplistic and primitive. Walter Werner and colleagues (1977) examine the multicultural content of and the pedagogy used in social studies curricula prescribed for elementary and secondary schools across Canada during the 1974-75 school year. The common approaches to teaching about Indian cultures at the time are described as "museum and heritage" at the elementary level and as "discipline and issues" at the secondary level. The former approaches, which I would have labelled "arts and crafts" (e.g., colour a totem pole made from an egg carton), tended to reinforce stereotypes because of the superficial treatment of culture. With the "discipline" approach, Indian people became objects of study. The "issues" often focused on the so-called "Indian problem." These same approaches were what I had experienced as a student at least fifteen years earlier. Learning about Indian cultures through the public school curriculum was something that I endured. Perhaps this was why I was drawn to developing better curricula about First Nations through teacher education and later as a teacher. I didn't want other First Nations children to suffer the same humiliation that I had experienced.

I admit, as a teacher, to using basal readers that had an Indian legend or two in them, but I supplemented these with other culturally based material that I found or developed. There was not much available, especially any developed by First Nations. I did not realize the significance of stories at the time, but I did feel that using an Indian legend to teach reading, particularly comprehension skills, was not appropriate. Dissecting the story for the purpose of developing a list of comprehension questions, to be discussed first in a question-and-answer format and then in writing, felt wrong. I did not hear traditional stories being told when I was a child; however, I did hear many life-experience stories. Not until I started working with the Coqualeetza Cultural Centre, the Stó:lō Sitel curriculum project, and the Elders' Group did I begin learning about the educational importance of stories.

In 1975 I became part of the Stó:lō Sitel Advisory Committee, which oversaw the development of the Stó:lō Sitel curriculum. The committee comprised ten to fifteen educators from the public school districts, band schools, Stó:lō communities, and Coqualeetza staff, all of whom met on a monthly basis. The committee developed curriculum policies, gave feedback on the curriculum approach and materials, and liaised with school administrators, teachers, and Stó:lō community members. The Advisory Committee and Elders' Group were the vital community link to the curriculum project. The Elders' Group became the "backbone" of the Stó:lō Sitel curriculum. The group provided the cultural knowledge, guided the process of development, and verified all material before it was published.[2] I also became one of the curriculum developers and, later, senior consultant to the curriculum project. The curriculum-development group included a coordinator, an artist, language and culture specialists, a writer, and a secretary. The process of working with the Elders and their stories included first getting their support and establishing their trust in the Stó:lō Sitel staff, tape-recording the Elders telling their stories, transcribing them, and finally putting the stories into text and developing illustrations for storybooks.

The need for the Stó:lō Sitel curriculum was first suggested by the Elders. They wanted their weekly meetings to focus on documenting cultural knowledge, but they didn't want the tape recorder used. I wondered whether this was because they didn't feel comfortable with the technology. Shirley Leon, the Coqualeetza Cultural Centre's manager, recalls that "every meeting we would bring the tape recorder, but they didn't want it turned on. It was at least eight months before they finally said at one meeting it was okay to turn the recorder on" (personal communication, 31 January 1996). She felt that the Elders needed to be reassured that those working on the documentation of cultural knowledge and the Stó:lō Sitel curriculum had the same intentions and motives as they did – the work was for the children and future generations. During this process, the written version of each story, its illustrations, and the accompanying teacher's lesson plan were verified with the Elder who had told the story.

I'm not sure why the printed text was selected as the main medium to represent the stories, aside from the fact that books were and are the predominant tool for instruction. Perhaps we wanted to legitimize First Nations stories through a literate form in school curricula. The Coqualeetza Cultural Centre was beginning to use video for some cultural programs, but developing them for school use was too expensive. Preparing the written/illustrated texts was time consuming; some stories took a full year to go through the developmental/printing process. The Elders were adamant about getting the story texts right, as Shirley Leon recalls: "[The Elders] would correct how their story was written. They would say, I didn't say that, you're putting words in my mouth ... that's not how I said it" (transcript, 5 December 1995).

The curriculum team developed one or two stories for Grades 1 to 4 in the manner described earlier. The stories that the Elders selected for inclusion in the Stó:lō Sitel curriculum contained information about cultural traditions, environmental knowledge, and values concerning interrelationships among people, nature, and land. The Elders' stories were then matched with the concepts of family, community, and culture prescribed by the Ministry of Education for teaching social studies at each grade level. The curriculum developers added a contextual introduction to the stories explaining that Stó:lō children heard stories from a grandparent either at bedtime or when they demonstrated disrespectful behaviour or broke a cultural rule. Hearing stories from grandparents at night or when one misbehaved resonates with traditional story ways.

The Elders were careful with the selection of stories appropriate for children. The ones that they shared were those that they had heard as children. For one of the grade levels, we wanted a story about plants, but the Elders would not give one. At first, we thought that they did not remember; however, they told us much later, after we had moved onto a different unit, that the stories they knew about plants were not to be told to children, as these stories had powerful knowledge about plants' medicinal, healing, or spiritual use that was too strong for children. At the time, I thought they meant only that children would not understand such stories, or that their content/language was too difficult for the children to understand, or that the stories would not interest children. I did not understand that power is embedded in some of the stories.

During the weekly discussion sessions with the Coqualeetza Elders' Group, the curriculum staff also asked questions about the age-level appropriateness of each story, about the meanings or teachings of each story, and about how these meanings or teachings were and should be presented through the use of story. During this research phase, as we called it, I learned to have patience and to wait for an answer when asking Elders questions. In the large group meetings, I recall at first feeling intimidated going before the Elders and asking questions because I didn't know them, hadn't done research in this manner, and I wasn't sure how to talk to them in a culturally respectful way. Now, I realize that I wasn't culturally ready to work with the Elders at the time. I had sat in on their meetings and observed the seriousness with which they approached the documentation of the Halq'emeylem language and cultural information with the linguist who was then working for Coqualeetza. I started by saying which reserve and which family I belonged to. Among the Stó:lō it is still customary to say where and which family you come from if the Elders don't know you so that those listening can place you within your community/family history. Identifying one in relation to place and family is part of knowing how one fits within the collective or larger cultural group, which is part of the holistic Indigenous framework.

I remember that often there were long silences after I asked my questions. At first, I was uncomfortable with these long silences and wondered whether the Elders didn't understand my questions or didn't want to answer. Sometimes, Shirley Leon would help by asking individuals to share their experiences in relation to a question. I learned that these silences were important because the Elders were thinking about the questions and preferred not speak until they were sure about their answers. Silence is respectful and can create good thinking. They would answer with stories of personal, family, and community experience. Sometimes, a question was not answered when it was asked because the Elders needed time to reawaken their memories and ensure that what they said was the truth as they knew it. They recognized that the work they were doing was a part of recording "oral history." Because it was for educational purposes, the cultural knowledge had to be accurate. Shirley Leon links the effect of taking time to think and talk about cultural knowledge to the process of making meaning from stories:

> I think Elders [who] were born storytellers weren't spontaneous decision makers ... I think that came from the history of the stories; you don't make up your mind [quickly]; you have to think about it ... maybe two, three days ... Some of our [curriculum] questions, we [had] to wait three, four weeks before we got answers. I think that's something we have to remember in today's life ... everything is so fast-paced, Elders are starting to say, "At least talk about things, especially where the language is concerned, don't you change anything unless you talk about it for at least six months." (Transcript, 5 December 1995)

The directive to spend more time talking about knowledge that is important has implications for researchers and educators who want and need particular knowledge immediately. The Elders understand that traditional forms of knowledge contained in the Halq'emeylem language and in their stories need to be carefully transformed into English and into current educational practice. We must also recognize that those who have the cultural knowledge often have to remember what they were told years earlier, that sometimes there is a translation process that occurs from the Halq'emeylem language into English, and that the Elders may not have thought about the topic of inquiry for years. I have often heard the Elders say that much of what they know about traditional knowledge was "put to sleep" – was not talked about. Ceremonial knowledge was also "outlawed" with the banning of cultural ceremonies in Canada from 1884 to 1951.

Today, discourse on Aboriginal education often speaks about the need to decolonize our perspectives and experiences by critiquing the impacts of Western education on Indigenous cultures and education (Battiste 2000, Royal Commission on Aboriginal Peoples 1996b, Smith 1999). In taking a different perspective, Graham Smith (2000), a scholar of Maōri ancestry, challenges us to examine the political struggles inherent in the educational sites where Western and Indigenous education meet. He emphasizes achieving an Indigenous consciousness-raising process that does not dwell on the colonizers but focuses on how Indigenous thought and action become transformative, thereby serving to improve Indigenous living conditions. I believe that the Elders' reminder to us to take time to talk in order to ensure correct representation of their Indigenous knowledge is an example of engaging in both decolonization and transformative-action processes. Through these processes we go back to important cultural principles that have survived colonization attempts in order to maintain Indigenous knowledge that will facilitate the type of transformative action that Smith advocates. Maybe the rabbit who has the responsibility to pass on cultural knowledge in the story "Coyote's Eyes," presented in Chapter 1, shows us what can happen if we don't critically engage in a decolonization or transformative-action process.

In the case of Stó:lō storytelling, no written sources exist that describe or analyze how people became storytellers and how story listening and the making of story meaning occurred. There are Stó:lō stories that anthropologists, linguists, and Stó:lō storytellers have published. The researcher/educator – who is also a learner – must establish a trusting teaching-learning relationship with those who know about storytelling, and she/he must learn the cultural implications embedded in the talk of the Elders. Wapaskwan's statement about the importance of knowing the implicit meanings of a (con)text or story rings true. An example would be the term "longhouse," which refers to a place where particular ceremonies and values are practised. Elders will not explicate the term's meaning because they assume that you know or feel that you ought to know what they mean. If you do not know what they mean, then there is an expectation that you will take responsibility for finding out. At one time, asking direct questions about what one said was considered rude. One reason for this relates to making meaning from stories, a process that involves going away to think about their meanings in relation to one's life. Today, Elders know that many Stó:lō people do not know the traditions, so they are willing to explain more. Some are used to talking to various people about cultural ways and have found methods to explain cultural meanings.

A deeper level of story meaning first occurred to me during a discussion at an Elders' meeting about the story "Mink and Miss Pitch," which was told by Susan Jimmie. It is one of the many stories in which Mink looks for a wife. I summarize it here.

MINK AND MISS PITCH

Mink is a Trickster character journeying to find a wife. He often picks beautiful but unavailable women and wants to marry them immediately. Mink usually has trouble because of his quick pick. Miss Pitch is the new object of Mink's attention and desire. Mink tries to persuade Miss Pitch to marry him by saying that he will look after all her needs. She lets Mink get close to her one night but turns down his marriage proposal the next day because she implies that they are too different to have a good marriage. She then ignores him. Mink won't take "no" for an answer and gets angry, then violent, with Miss Pitch when he can't have his way. He hits Miss Pitch with one arm, then the other, and kicks her with one foot, then the other. Then he butts her with his forehead and gets stuck to her pitchiness, overnight, in this awkward position. The next day, when the sun warms Miss Pitch, she releases Mink, knowing that she has made her point. Mink goes away. His search continues.

The Elders related some of their understandings from this story: the problems of intermarriage, the cyclical effects of violence, and the need to challenge relationships because of major differences. At this moment, as the reader, you are invited to join the story circle in order to add your meanings gleaned from this story.

Before this discussion, I didn't like the story because of Mink's violence. I saw no humour in the story, yet the Elders said that it was a humorous story. My understanding was stuck on spousal abuse. After listening to the Elders' discussion, I began to think beyond the physical violence and about cultural and racial differences, particularly about problems resulting from these differences. I started using this story in Stó:lō Sitel workshops with educators, usually reading the text version at the end of the workshop. I did this because I wasn't comfortable or confident enough to tell the story. I used the story to reinforce points introduced during the workshop, especially those where difficulties occurred when people with opposing views and attitudes encountered one another. I would hint at these meanings by personalizing them in this manner: "Sometimes I feel like Miss Pitch wanting to ignore and to keep people away who have differing views or who are aggressive in wanting the quick and easy approach to teaching Aboriginal students." From these workshops, I realized that people connected with this story on an emotional level; some shared their experiences of encountering interpersonal differences.

I gradually became more familiar and comfortable with this story and began to appreciate its humorous aspects. Imagining Mink as he physically clings to Miss Pitch in his "sticky" predicament as a result of his disrespectful behaviour and selfish thinking is funny. The Elders know Mink as a Trickster character who gets into many difficult situations, and they can laugh at and with Mink. I now appreciate that Miss Pitch simultaneously exercised power and experienced difficulty in saying "no." When Aboriginal people say "no" to aspects of Western education that clash with our cultural knowledge and ways of knowing, we often feel assaulted by the continued pressure to conform through new forms of colonization, such as government policies and procedures. But like Miss Pitch, we stand upon the ground – the land – of our cultural knowledge, which has sustained us since time immemorial: we prevail.

In 1981 I took a break from the Stó:lō Sitel curriculum project to work as a First Nations studies instructor and then as the co-ordinator and later the supervisor for the Native Indian Teacher Education Program (NITEP) at the University of British Columbia. The concept of the emotional and healing power of story became more real to me as I learned to tell stories in a new context with First Nations adult learners enrolled in a university program.

Living the Power of Story

When I began working for the NITEP, I used First Nations stories in classes that I taught and in educational talks that I gave in a manner similar to that described in the Stó:lō Sitel curriculum project. I gradually gained the confidence and ability to remember and tell stories without using a written text. Before 1990 I had not trained my memory to retain these stories; perhaps this was due to my reliance on the literate form and to my lack of confidence in telling stories. I began to remember humorous stories, mostly about Coyote, and I consciously used my memory more and used writing less when listening to lectures and when recalling phone numbers and even grocery lists. This memory-building exercise revealed how much I and today's ways of living rely so heavily on the use of literacy. The story "Coyote's Eyes" was a fun way to try to learn the balance of which Terry Tafoya spoke. I would imagine seeing the world only through the lens of the oral way and through use of the memory, only to realize how unskilled I was and how few people live this way today. The Elders are those most familiar and skilled with orality. They also read, but they recount cultural knowledge and history through orally told stories. There are some whose oral accounts are rich in detail about events, dates, names, and places.

Then I would switch to the literate lens and appreciate its archival function and the opportunity to rest the memory and listening functions for a while. Having the typed transcriptions of the Elders' talks and stories gave me a feeling of security, as I knew that I could keep going back to them to complete a thematic analysis and to get necessary detail. Talking, hearing, and feeling during my personal interactions with the Elders as well as visualizing their stories during and after our sessions helped me to establish some thematic notions that were verified by their textual record. The written record of their stories lacks the nuances of our interpersonal interaction and the depth of the emotion and humour that were shared. Because the oral process, unlike the written record, involves the listeners' memories, it is limited by what the listeners can recall and later share with others. Used together, orality and literacy find a mutually beneficial meeting place where each has a function that contributes to increased understanding of storytelling. I was beginning to value the function, or worldview, of each of Coyote's mismatched eyes, so to speak.

The stories that I really remembered were ones that I did not set out to consciously try to remember, and they came from both oral and written sources. They were ones with which I instantly and strongly connected on an emotional level first. But I also connected with them physically, intellectually, and spiritually. Something that the characters experienced in each of these stories grabbed me emotionally. When I say that I connected with them physically, I mean that I reflected on behaviours and actions of mine that needed changing or that needed to be practised more. My imagination was challenged to visualize the stories' plots and characters and to think about the possible meanings of the stories. It was as though these stories became embedded in my body, in my emotional being, in my consciousness, and in my spirit. My experience differs from that of some other scholars who have worked with

Indigenous storytellers in an attempt to understand the power of stories to help one to live a good life. Here, I will digress for a moment to illustrate this point.

Keith Basso's work with the Western Apache uses a hunting metaphor to show how stories told to someone may "hit" her/him purposefully in order to "promote compliance with standards for acceptable social behavior" (1996, 41). In the words of Western Apache consultant Nick Thompson:

> It's like an arrow, they say. Sometimes it just bounces off – it's too soft and you don't think about anything. But when it's strong it goes in deep and starts working on your mind right away. No one says anything to you, only that story is all, but now you know that people have been watching you and talking about you. They don't like how you've been acting. So you have to think about your life. (Quoted in Basso 1996, 58-59)

Nick Thompson says that the land in the Western Apache territory "looks after us. The land keeps badness away" (61) because its stories and place names are essentially good: "they make you remember how to live right, so you want to replace [heal] yourself again" (59). Perhaps the way that some stories pierced my consciousness is similar to the action described by Elder Nick Thompson. As a beginning storyteller/teacher, I received a few stories that became part of my heart knowledge. When telling stories for educational purposes, at first I spent time planning which story to tell, then I developed my talk around the story.

Gradually, the process of my planning which story to tell in order to illustrate some meaning changed to one in which I let my intuitive nature select the story to be told. Instead of planning which story to use and framing my talk around the story, I waited to get some feeling from the group or the situation or waited until a particular story came into my mind and being – wanting to be told. I have heard other storytellers say that they will not know exactly which story will come out until moments before they are to speak. It is the storytelling situation and the needs of the people that guide the selection of story in these circumstances. Knowing the stories intimately, as though they are a part of one's being, is essential if a storyteller is to use her/his intuitive sense for telling stories. The thoughts of the late Harry Robinson mean more to me now. He was told by his grandmother that to remember a story you must "Write it on your heart" (Wickwire and Robinson 1989, 28).

I remember a time, 4 February 1992, when I was to tell a story to a small group of third- and fourth-year NITEP students enrolled in an educational seminar. Sheila TeHenneppe, the instructor and my friend, wanted a story that could be used for the term's seminar sessions. Her plan was that I would tell the same story at the beginning and end of the term. I went to the classroom early before anyone arrived, waited, and asked for guidance from the Creator. When selecting a story to tell, I had come to rely on this practice of getting a sense of the place and people and asking for this type of help. It was a beautiful spring-like day, the windows were open, and upon hearing the birds' songs, I knew which story to tell. This session was my first powerful emotional healing experience with story, where the story took on a "life" and became the teacher.

We put our chairs in a circle. Sheila introduced me and then gave me a jar of home-canned pears to symbolize the act of feeding the storyteller, a symbol of reciprocity, which Leslie Marmon Silko, of Pueblo ancestry, talks about: "That's what you're supposed to do, you know, you're supposed to feed the storyteller good things" (1981, 110). Then I told the story "The Bird in the Tree."[3]

THE BIRD IN THE TREE

There were two male cousins; one lived in a northern
isolated part of BC, and the other in the city of Vancouver.
One day, the northern cousin came to visit his city cousin.
   The city fellow wanted to bring his cousin to the better,
more lively parts of Vancouver. He chose Robson Street.
Robson Street gets quite busy with lots of people walking
along the street, shopping and looking around. There's lots
of traffic, loud music being played from the car stereos. As
they were walking down Robson Street, the northern
fellow said, "I feel out of place here. This cement sidewalk
is so hard, my feet are sore from walking on it. There are so
many people, you get bumped a lot. It's so noisy. I miss my
home. I miss the quiet. I miss the smell of the land. I miss
the trees and mountains being close by, and I miss the
birds' songs. I feel as out of place here as that bird I hear
singing in a tree at the end of the street."
   The city cousin said, "You must be homesick: how can
you hear a bird singing in a tree at the end of the street
with all this noise?" The northern cousin said, "Let me

show you something. Do you have any coins?" The city
fellow handed him a pocketful of change. The northern
cousin took it and threw the coins onto the cement.

A strange thing happened as those coins hit the sidewalk.
There was a moment of silence. In that moment of silence,
the people and their noise stopped. In that moment of
silence, those who listened heard a bird singing in a tree at
the end of the street.

After telling the story, I asked the participants to say whatever they
wanted in relation to the story. I also asked them to hold a small rock
while speaking; they could also choose not to hold it. I said that for me
the rock serves as a reminder of our connection to the earth and serves
as a "witness" to what is said. Our people, the Stó:lō, believe that rocks
come from a life form – the earth – and have a lifeforce within. In many
of our stories, transformations occur between humans and forms of
nature, such as rocks. Rocks can be like our relations, like family members, who listen to us. As each person began talking about how she/he
related to the story or about what it meant to her/him, the power of the
moment seemed to keep on building. Each personal story connected
deeply, on an emotional level, with each person around the circle. Some
cultural songs were shared.

Because the experience became an important turning point that created an important realization, I asked Sheila TeHenneppe and two of
the participants, Floy Pepper, an Elder originally from the Creek Indian
Nation of Oklahoma, and Shirley Sterling, of the Nlha7kapmx (Interior
Salish) Nation, to reflect on this experience, their perceptions about
the power of story, and this particular storytelling session. They readily
agreed because they remembered the powerful effects of the experience,
although its details had faded by the time I asked them, almost four
years later. As Shirley Sterling said: "Sometimes I have a hard time remembering what I said yesterday" (transcript, 7 February 1996).

During the conversation Shirley said that she remembered the bird
imagery from the story vividly because she was reminded of her father's
affinity for birds. Sheila, who is non-Native, had worked with NITEP
students for twelve years and had gained cultural understandings from
interactions with the students and other First Nations. When I used the
term "power of story," Sheila and Shirley each identified this power as
the story having its own life:

We didn't know what was going to happen ... I remember [one of the participants] was hurting [emotionally, spiritually] and somehow it [the story] took care of her and [then] all of us ... I'd say [this story] had a life of its own. (Sheila TeHenneppe, transcript, 3 November 1995)

I've always had that sense that stories have their own life ... because sometimes when you tell a story to a hunter, the hunter will take, interpret that story differently than say the basket maker. And the basket maker may remember other details. So the story takes on a life of its own and it travels from person to person and it ... takes a different shape, but there's something the same. Each person interprets slightly differently and yet it's really amazing how some stories will persist ... [for years]. (Shirley Sterling, transcript, 17 February 1996)

From the way that Shirley talked about the story, it is evident that she believed it has a "life," even though she is aware that story listeners will shape a story to their situations. This "life" derives from a story's core values, or teachings, which keep the story going and useful to people.

Sheila also believed, and I agree, that the use of the circle, rock, and food establishes respectful contextual signals that say,

this is a time to sit together ... The rock, the circle, represents a certain kind of behaviour, and people in the circle know that something can be brought into the circle to do. These signals mean that things are going to go in a particular way ... [They] open up a way for the story [to be] put into the circle, and it goes from there. (Transcript, 3 November 1995)

In this particular storytelling experience, the way of sharing was open-ended. Shirley's relationship to the story "The Bird in the Tree" had a powerful healing effect on me, for I gained appreciation of a story's impact on another person.

She said that last night she was feeling very lonely. Her home was in northern BC, and she was missing her family and was finding it hard getting used to living in the city. She called home. Her mother answered and she could not talk about her sadness; she could not say anything; she could only cry. Then her mother started to sing her some traditional songs. That was all she did, little else was said. At the session, the student said she felt better after hearing those songs. The bird's song reminded her of the healing effect of her mother's songs. (Fieldnote, 5 February 1992)

Floy Pepper shared her memory of how the rock that was sent around the circle took on its own power:

All right, for the first time in my life I had to hold a rock that felt like it was alive ... I don't know where the feeling came from; it was like from the story. But ... as I handled the rock it was ... like I had something alive in my hands. I've never felt a rock that felt that way before ... It was almost as if it had vibes. So I associated [the rock] with the powerful thing that happened there.

As Floy and I talked further, she remembered the strong spiritual feeling that increased with each person's words and/or songs:

To me it was sort of a spirituality thing, and then when Shirley sang her song, that really got me because I'd been through a disastrous period during that time. I thought that whole experience that afternoon was really ... uplifting ... It was like something great happened ... As I reflect back ... I can recall [those] feelings. [Shirley] ... recorded that song for me, when I play it I still get the same kind of feeling you know. (Transcript, 9 January 1996)

The storytelling experience of 5 February 1992 made me understand what others have said about stories and about the talk associated with them, which is that stories have an ability to soothe, to heal. In this session, the story and the storytelling context enabled the participants to interact with the story, to let it help them bring out emotional concerns so that others could then help. This particular story has been heard by Sheila a number of times in different contexts. She shared an experience in which "The Bird in the Tree" again "became a life of its own" and created "a place ... a reality" to interact through story.

One day, only a couple of months ago, I was walking downtown, on Hastings Street, with a friend and chatting. It was still warm, it was a nice day and another friend of ours came running out of one of the buildings ... she was visibly upset ... She was startled to see us, so we talked. She didn't want to say what was wrong, but she said she would be okay in a minute, but for that moment she was not okay ... We talked to her, to see if she wanted to go for a walk, go have coffee.

This is the part I can't explain, but it happened. It was like that place on the street, was so clear, somehow we were inside a bubble ... nothing else was going on, but you know how busy Hastings Street is. [This] zone has three people in it; it was really quiet. The friend that I was with reached down on the ground and picked up a maple leaf, a fall maple leaf. It was not fall. [She] gave it to the woman that was upset ... there was a little tree ... standing next to us which we hadn't noticed. Our friend took [the leaf], it was like a treasure, something to take care of her and she left.

Both my friend and I were thinking of your story, totally. It was like we were inside the story ... It was like being an actor in the story ... all of a sudden [there] was silence ... It was like that same [story] space opened up. We could say to each other, it was exactly like Jo-ann's story ... a silence was created, it was a spiritual silence for me. I hadn't ... actually connected to that part of the bird story before. I felt the silence. It wasn't money on the ground, it was a beautiful leaf, that leaf was a gift ... Later on [we saw this same woman] at an event, and she felt much better and was appreciative of that beautiful moment. I can't articulate it well, [but] it was like living out that story. (Transcript, 3 November 1995)

After the NITEP storytelling experience, I began to wonder about the potential of the power in story to heal the emotions and spirit. "The Bird in the Tree" isn't a traditional First Nations story, but it became my story to use in a cultural way that enabled people to interact with a story and each other through a storywork process. I also wondered whether this was one way that stories became attributed to particular storytellers. If so, then which cultural rules apply to this story? Because I am Stó:lō, does "The Bird in the Tree" become a Stó:lō story, or am I appropriating someone else's story?[4]

As I return to this particular question sometime later, I am nudged to rethink the emotional and spiritual healing process that occurred. Aboriginal people living in the city can feel alienated from their home territories or dislocated from their traditional teachings in a Western-dominated environment. The use of Indigenous traditional knowledge such as that found in story, song, and speech provided a framework for the contemporary story to work for the group.

The important point of my relating this story experience is that the power created during the storytelling session seemed interrelational as it moved among the storyteller and story listeners in the storytelling situation. This interaction created a synergistic story power that had emotional, healing, and spiritual aspects. This synergistic story power also brought the story "to life." Becoming a storyteller and experiencing the power of storywork gave me more confidence to work with story in an educational curriculum designed for school-age students.

CHAPTER FIVE

Storywork in Action

If Coyote with the mismatched eyes had spent time with the Stó:lō and Coast Salish Elders, he would have learned that to see clearly from the eye of the oral tradition, he needed to understand the cultural ways that stories were told and taught to children, that storytellers learned the stories not only from master storytellers but also by being closely connected to land, that stories can become a teacher, and that we can live life through stories. As Coyote continues with me on this journey, he tries to use his eyes to see how Indigenous stories can be transformed into an educational curriculum for children. But in this story a major challenge is that now one eye is shaped by the Canadian justice system, the courts in particular, and the other eye is shaped by the oral traditions of First Nations peoples.

This chapter presents a practical application of First Nations storywork in a provincial elementary-level (kindergarten to Grade 7) school curriculum. The First Nations Journeys of Justice curriculum project was developed under the auspices of the Law Courts Education Society of British Columbia (LCES). The foundation of information and analysis for this chapter comes from interviews with curriculum staff, self-reflection, fieldnotes, reports, minutes of meetings, curriculum documents, and teaching material. This curriculum included other components besides First Nations stories; however, only experiences related to storywork are examined here. This chapter illustrates multiple dimensions of the practical application of the storywork principles of respect, responsibility, reciprocity, and reverence with and by community-based storytellers.

Getting Started: The Curriculum Planning and Development Process of Years One and Two

The LCES, a public legal-education organization, had a province-wide mandate:

> With the vision of building bridges between the First Nations and Canadian systems of law, this education program honours orality [storytelling] – a traditional approach to education among First Nations of British Columbia – and teaches concepts and practices of justice from the perspective of First Nations ways of knowing. (LCES 1994a, "Mission Statement," 1)

I was appointed to the board of directors of the Law Courts Education Society in 1989 as a First Nations representative with experience and interest in educational programming. In 1990 a five-member First Nations Advisory Committee, which I chaired, was established to ensure broader representation of First Nations concerns and experiences with the justice system.

The different views of justice presented by Aboriginal cultures and the Canadian court system are like the two different eyes in the story "Coyote's Eyes."[1] Associate Chief Judges A.C. Hamilton and C.M. Sinclair conducted an inquiry into the administration of justice for Aboriginal people in Manitoba. They reinforce the different meanings that justice has for Aboriginal cultures and the "dominant society":

> The dominant society tries to control actions it considers potentially or actually harmful to society as a whole, to individuals or to the wrongdoers themselves by interdiction, enforcement or apprehension, in order to prevent or punish harmful or deviant behaviour. The emphasis is on the punishment of the deviant as a means of making that person conform, or as a means of protecting other members of society.
>
> The purpose of a justice system in an Aboriginal society is to restore the peace and equilibrium within the community, and to reconcile the accused with his or her own conscience and with the individual or family who has been wronged. This is a primary difference. It is a difference that significantly challenges the appropriateness of the present

legal and justice system for Aboriginal people in the resolution of conflict, the reconciliation and the maintenance of community harmony and good order. (1991, 22)

The Advisory Committee on which I sat acknowledged these differences. Its members felt that an understanding of First Nations traditional concepts of justice was needed by students and teachers. They recommended the development of a province-wide elementary school curriculum that uses First Nations stories to show that we have concepts of justice.

The co-operation and involvement of Aboriginal community members and organizations was a fundamental principle and practice of the curriculum work. The Advisory Committee believed that with community involvement and local adaptation to the curriculum, Aboriginal children would learn more about their culture in a positive manner. The committee members also wanted the curriculum to be useful to the community as a resource for further developing its own youth-justice initiatives. The curriculum was to be for First Nations band and public schools.

It took a year before funding was secured from eight different sources. Three staff were hired by October 1992: one co-ordinator and two researchers/curriculum writers. My responsibilities for this project included leading the development of the philosophical approach, the scope and sequence, and the storywork approach. A Teachers' Advisory Committee was established that comprised seven First Nations educators from various band and urban public schools. Among these educators, some of whom had been classroom teachers, were a cultural co-ordinator, a curriculum developer, a district co-ordinator of First Nations education, a district principal, a support worker who helped teachers with First Nations curriculum and provided services to students, and a band councillor. The curriculum team felt that an Elder for the project was essential, someone who could give guidance to the staff when necessary. Dr. Ellen White was approached because she is a gifted storyteller who has worked in elementary schools, published some of her stories, and participated in community-based justice initiatives. She willingly agreed to be the project Elder. The Native Advisory Committee and the Teacher's Advisory Committee (NACTAC) were joined for the five meetings held over the two-year period.

The first six months of year one (October 1992 to March 1993) were devoted to the planning phase, which focused on collecting research literature, examining existing First Nations-oriented curricula, contacting various resource people for ideas, and achieving a consensus, through many group meetings, about the philosophical rationale, a scope and sequence, and possible unit themes. The task of developing a school curriculum for eight grade levels that includes First Nations storytelling, First Nations and Canadian forms of justice, and community involvement had not been done before in North America. The task seemed overwhelming, problematic, yet exciting. During the second half of year one (April 1993 to September 1993), the work focused on the development of the first draft of the curriculum prototype (philosophy, scope and sequence, units, and lessons, with accompanying stories), which was verified with the NACTAC.

In year two the curriculum work of the first six months (October 1993 to March 1994) included more detailed development of the lessons and accompanying teaching materials, reviewing these with the NACTAC and others within the justice system, beginning a series of revisions based on feedback, identifying potential pilot schools, and gaining these schools' agreement to pilot the curriculum. The last six months of year two (April 1994 to September 1994) was spent on curriculum piloting, revisions, and final preparation for print-ready copy. Professional-development teacher workshops at the pilot schools included some preparation for storytelling, which was further developed as a section in each grade level's "Teacher's Guide." The pilot project was completed in four schools from April to June 1994. The print material was revised, graphics and photos were selected, and a storytelling video was developed. The curriculum was published and launched on 29 September 1994.

Creating Opportunities for Community Involvement

A major aspect of the work of the Law Courts Education Society has been to establish partnerships with various groups of people. The metaphor of building bridges was used in the early stages of the First Nations Journeys of Justice curriculum project to create links for partnerships and for community involvement:

> The proposed project is grounded in the belief that a bridge can be built to develop common understandings between First Nations and mainstream Canadian peoples, but that the footings for that bridge on the First Nations side must rest on solid cultural wisdom. The proposed curriculum would aim at strengthening cultural values and building

self-esteem as bedrock for broader educational developments. This objective will be accomplished in part through involving the community in the development of the curricula, and through attention paid to the "interconnectedness" of all aspects of the learning process. (LCES 1991, 8)

The curriculum approach was built upon the principles of local control and community involvement advocated by the 1972 national policy Indian Control of Indian Education, which was developed by the national Aboriginal political organization of the time, the National Indian Brotherhood. This educational policy, adopted by the federal government, has influenced First Nations education throughout Canada.[2] From 1992 to 1994 a curriculum team of five people worked with approximately one hundred storytellers, educators, cultural-centre personnel, tribal-council members, justice/court personnel, and funders to document and develop a justice curriculum for kindergarten to Grade 7 that combines First Nations traditional and life-experience stories with information about the Canadian justice/court system. Twelve First Nations organizations, bands, and tribal councils throughout British Columbia wrote letters of support and indicated a willingness to participate in this curriculum project. At least sixty Aboriginal people either shared their stories or were consulted about storywork. Fifteen British Columbia First Nations cultures are represented in the final version of the First Nations Journeys of Justice curriculum.

Bridging a Chasm

The curriculum team developed the philosophical approach based on an examination of the source of laws, the Indian Control of Indian Education policy, and the concept of holism. We were determined to base the curriculum on First Nations perspectives and then look for parallels from the Canadian justice system. An examination of the source of laws from both sides showed that a chasm exists:

Why do they seem to be so far apart? ... Rather than having justice as part of the internal structure of the community, as in First Nations societies, communities in northern European culture created external structures to carry out the work that needed to be done in the area of justice. Thus, the system of justice is external to the community, rather than internal. This is the model that was imported to Canada. (LCES 1994a, "Teacher's Guide," 14-15)

The external notion of justice is explained as follows: "The Canadian legal system has been separated from the rest of normal, everyday living, and much of how it works cannot be understood by the average person ... we need a lawyer to represent us in a court of law, someone who understands how the system works" (14). In contrast, in some Indigenous societies traditional law is internal, known, and embedded in cultural ways through stories and through ceremonies such as feasting/potlatching in which "rights" to territories or names may be given, exercised, and witnessed by the guests. Even though many First Nations follow their own cultural traditions as well as the laws of Canada, there is growing dissatisfaction with the justice/court system when First Nations traditional knowledge is denied as evidence:

> Western concepts of objectivity and fact make oral histories suspect and unreliable in the court's eyes. As demonstrated in the recent judgment of former British Columbia Supreme Court Chief Justice Allan McEachern (1991) in *Delgam Uukw v. HRMTQ*, Canadian legal institutions are fundamentally Eurocentric, allowing for little difference in cultural worldviews. (Pryce 1992, 35)

Finding similarities between the concepts of justice common to First Nations and the Canadian justice system was one approach to bridging the chasm used in the First Nations Journeys of Justice curriculum. Four major concepts were agreed upon: being safe, being responsible, being fair, and getting along. However, arriving at a consensus on these four common justice concepts did not occur until the curriculum was almost ready to be published.

The curriculum team and NACTAC members first identified ten traditional justice concepts that had important applications to First Nations: sharing, reciprocity, co-operation, respect, rights, the importance of caregivers, harmony, interdependence, honour, and balance. The group wanted the stories to exemplify these concepts. In fact, these concepts were verified during the meetings, as individuals often told traditional or life-experience stories related either to what they believed justice was traditionally or to what they believed it should be. The ten concepts were embedded in the stories subsequently selected for the curriculum and were developed in the lesson activities. But some of the educators in the field of non-First Nations justice felt strongly that the categories of concepts should not be collapsed in this way, preferring that the curriculum explicitly show the sequential development of the concepts throughout the grade-level units and how they were incorporated in a "practical and useable" curriculum format (LCES 1994a, "Teacher's Guide," 1).

During the revision process from June to August 1994, the four concepts of being safe, being responsible, being fair, and getting along were agreed upon, after much discussion, by the curriculum staff and the NACTAC. The ten traditional justice concepts were noted on each page of the scope and sequence so that they wouldn't be totally forgotten. First Nations artists designed logos that not only depicted the four common justice concepts but also encompassed the ten traditional justice concepts within the logos' meanings. Identifying and introducing concepts of justice that are common to both First Nations and the Canadian justice/court system was the workable[3] starting place for an elementary-level curriculum. And the principle of community involvement was the workable starting place for the development of storywork pedagogy.

Going to the People and Their Stories

In the staff planning sessions, some story types were identified as needed for particular unit themes. These included Trickster, origin, historical, naming, territorial, and life-experience stories. Also needed were stories that had First Nations teachings about working together, ensuring safety and security as a basic need and right, relationships with nature, and settling conflict. All of these were discussed with community storytellers (LCES 1992-94, 16-36). The important aspect of selecting stories was that the storytellers would be the ones to first identify the stories that they felt were appropriate and that they wanted used in the curriculum. The staff wanted a framework for discussing the purpose and area of need for each story in order to facilitate the work of identifying stories that the storytellers could share.

A constant constraint plaguing the project was one of time limitations. Three members of the curriculum team worked intensively and individually with storytellers and educators from at least fifteen First Nations groups to acquire appropriate stories for the curriculum. Each person agreed to work in specific regional areas of the province. Names of storytellers or people who worked in cultural education were suggested by NACTAC members and by staff. Each of the three staff members contacted the storytellers or their liaison helpers or their tribal councils/organizations to identify local protocol procedures and to make arrangements for a visit during June 1993. Letters were sent requesting participants' permission. Sometimes, the staff member visited a community and attended an Elders' meeting arranged by a local contact person to request participation. After an explanation of the curriculum project, many individual storytellers gave their consent to participate. This was one important step in gaining acceptance by the world of the storytellers, but there were various obstacles to overcome in getting support and establishing a working relationship with storytellers.

As I learned during my research, Simon Baker, Vincent Stogan, Ellen White, and the Stó:lō Elders use personal life-experience stories as one way to teach others. They know that the person asking the questions does not have the knowledge needed to understand the topic of inquiry. It might seem that Elders are not directly answering or co-operating, even though they have agreed to help the person who asks. But they are answering and directing the learning process by providing life-experience stories that contain values, background or contextual information, and issues that one must know in order to make meaning through storywork. Creating time to listen and having patience to learn what storytellers are sharing and teaching are fundamental to establishing respectful relationships.

Establishing Relationships and Taking Direction from Elders

The co-operation and direction received from the many First Nations groups and individuals attests to their commitment to improving educational curricula with their cultural knowledge. The principle of respectful partnerships established by the LCES helped create the opportunity for people to work together. Being culturally "worthy" or "ready" is important to understanding the fundamental values of respect, reverence, responsibility, and reciprocity in relation to Indigenous storywork. As explained by the project co-ordinator, Noella Little Mustache, the cultural concept of enacting responsibility was essential to being culturally ready to work with Elders.

> I guess the key responsibility was honouring the Elder and being focused ... I found that the critical part was talking to them at their place. The other responsibility was a follow-up with the Elders; it's like the Elders did not [stay] a stranger to me, they became my friend. And I felt they shared part of me. I passed something onto the project, but I also felt some of those teachings stayed with me. And it was a gift. (Transcript, 3 July 1995)

The storyteller directed the place, timing, and pace of discussion. An Elder storyteller reinforced the importance of prayer, as an aspect of the cultural concept of reverence, before beginning storywork with Noella.

> I just came at lunch time and there was a gentleman cooking ... chili and fried bread, so I was invited. [M, the storyteller] was involved with her students, they were making birch-bark baskets, her grandchildren were coming and going. When it came time to be interviewed I waited for [M] until she was ready. I waited. I had all my bags sitting there and my tape recorder, and I would have liked to have said to her, "We should start at this time," but I had to wait for her, 'til she was ready. We started the interview but then after a while she said, "Let's go to this other building." Her extended family was coming and going.
>
> We went to the other building and that's when she said, "I should pray before we start" ... Most of the Elders that I interviewed started with a prayer and ended with a prayer, and it kept me feeling that I was at the right place at the right time. There was that feeling that the Creator brought us here together to give thanks [for what] we have eaten and also [to] give thanks that all First Nations people are still here. I felt very special. They themselves were gifted and I was in that sacred environment. So [M] sat there after the prayer and she was busy sewing. She sewed and she talked. (Transcript, 3 July 1995)

Sometimes, Noella explained, the conversation between the storyteller and curriculum worker introduced philosophical teachings that were subsequently used for the unit lessons:

> We talked a lot about residential schools and then she [the storyteller] said, "I need to talk about the circle of life." She stated that everything was the circle of life and said this has to be the foundation of your curriculum. She didn't say curriculum, but the work you have been talking about. And this circle of life is where she talks about the salmon. The life cycle of the salmon, she used that as a symbol, that the salmon when they go out, like us going out in life, learning and that life cycle will have to end ... and young children are born ... We finish, we've had our purpose in life but other people will carry that on. [Her] story of the sockeye gave me a lot of caring for the family, a lot of responsibility that we have ... there's a path in which people have to follow. She talked

about the 'male salmon helping the female and the eggs [being] made and there's a partnership, there's co-operation, and it's like she was saying that in our world we also have to have that. (Transcript, 3 July 1995)

This type of direction was very helpful to the curriculum researchers since they often were not familiar with the cultural ways of the individual storytellers. Much of this contextual information was included in the curriculum lessons.

The storytellers demonstrated respect and responsible care for their stories, and they were explicit about the representation of their stories. A consequence was dilemmas such as whether to insist on grammatical correctness, problems when a storyteller decided that a story was not ready to be published and denied its inclusion, and tensions over collective ownership of stories. The impetus to fix up a story so that it looks "better" on paper may come from the influences of school-based literacy. Fixing up a story may also change the "tone" of the story, as some Elders say. The principle of doing what the storytellers want with their stories may raise concerns about changing the form of the oral tradition. If a storyteller felt that a story wasn't ready to be put into textual form and published, she/he withdrew it. If a story is a collective one, the reasons for determining that it is not "ready" may include not having all the appropriate permissions from those who have authority to let the story be published. The storytellers' direction was followed by the curriculum staff. Each dilemma had to be worked out as it arose. There were many dilemmas that we had not anticipated. Ownership of stories and authority to tell stories are complex matters influenced not only by individual, family, and community considerations but by political ones as well.

Establishing a collaborative working relationship with community storytellers takes time and skill, as those involved must come to understand and agree on cultural and political protocol, which of course varies among Indigenous peoples. Maintaining a respectful and trusting relationship requires patience, open communication, the will to respond, and the ability to negotiate satisfactory solutions. To help teachers and others begin to form respectful relationships with First Nations community members, I produced a video that introduces considerations and examples of story pedagogy. I wanted teachers to see the storytellers, get to know more about their approaches to storytelling, and hear them tell their stories.

Introducing Storytelling through Video

The *Teacher's storytelling video* shows three storytellers, Ellen White, Jeff McNeil-Bobb, and Frank Brown, each of whom contributed to the curriculum. The video's purposes are (1) to provide more information about particular stories used in the curriculum, (2) to share considerations about teaching approaches and cultural protocol for First Nations stories, and (3) to act as a catalyst for teachers and community members wanting to engage in First Nations storywork (LCES 1994a, "Story Guide," 37-38).[4] Often, when I read stories by Indigenous storytellers, I long to hear their voices and see them telling the stories. Seeing and hearing a storyteller in action begins a process of interrelating that happens among listener, storyteller, and story. The video thus serves as a secondary source for this interpersonal dimension and context for working with stories. Teachers may use some of the questions posed, information shared, and issues raised as beginning points for dialogue with First Nations storytellers and/or community members.

Ellen White, Jeff McNeil-Bobb, and Frank Brown talked with me about their stories and their philosophy about storywork, made suggestions about using these stories in the classroom, and told a story or two. Our conversations were put into written-transcript format. I edited them and sent them to each person for changes and approval before the final video edits were completed. This video, along with each grade level's "Teacher's Guide," was intended to give the teacher introductory information about the nature of First Nations stories, beginning pedagogy for storywork, and ideas for collaborative work with local community educators/storytellers.

Each of the three contributed in a different way. Jeff McNeil-Bobb is from the Stó:lō Nation and has worked as a teacher, artist, curriculum developer, cultural/language co-ordinator, and band councillor. I had known Jeff, who was also a member of the NACTAC, since 1983. I chose to portray his philosophical views about the nature of stories and to include an example of his use of story metaphor in order to present the questionable issue of explicating meaning for children. The goal was to show that there are differences of opinion about aspects of storywork.

When I asked Jeff where the story that he contributed came from, he recalled learning some stories from his grandfather, which were told to him as story "segments." Jeff put these segments into one story for the curriculum project. This use of story demonstrates the way that a younger generation of storytellers may change the traditional way of using stories to suit a contemporary learning context. Of particular interest is his statement about gaining understandings in his adult years:

> There was always parts of the day when I would be hurt, woeful, and be curled up somewhere. And he [my grandfather] would come over and ask, "What is wrong?" Generally, out of those things, something [a story] would come out. Back then, each one of them was in a segment of its own, but in reflection, I'm now just beginning to understand some things he said. (Personal communication, July 1994)

Stories told to young children, either in circumstances such as Jeff's or at bedtime, which was the case for some of the Stó:lō Elders, may have served at the time to sooth emotions or to teach about behaviour. The same stories heard over and over again become embedded in one's being, staying there until reflection in one's later years brings adult understandings and sometimes enables one to become a storyteller. Making meaning from a particular story can happen at various phases of human development; the meaning may change over time.

· Stories, then, have a way of "living," of being perpetuated both by the listener/learner's way of making meaning and by the storytellers, who have an important responsibility to tell stories in a particular way. Ellen White said, "Our lives are stories ... Storytellers have to be very responsible. They are setting the pace of breathing. A story is, and has, breath. Storytellers learn to let that happen" (LCES 1994a, "Teacher's Guide," 49-50). I believe that Ellen is talking about the power of story to "be the teacher," which is a storywork pedagogy.

A synergistic action happens between the storyteller and story, but it is the storyteller who ultimately gives breath, or life, to the story. From listening to and reading what storytellers say about making meaning from story, I have learned that the traditional ways favour no or very little direct guidance from the storyteller. However, the effects of colonization, assimilation, and acculturation, predominantly through schooling, have left many people unable to engage in story listening and to make story meaning, unless directly guided.

Learning from Life-Experience Stories

Many First Nations storytellers use their personal life experiences as teaching stories in a manner similar to how they use traditional stories. These storytellers help to carry on the oral tradition's obligation of educational reciprocity. One such storyteller is Frank Brown, of the Heiltsuk Nation,

Waglisla (Bella Bella), British Columbia. He talked about producing a video, *The voyage of rediscovery,* which is about his life-experience story. Included in the curriculum project as "The Frank Brown Story," this life-experience story is used with third-grade students, who learn that Frank got into trouble as a youth for robbery and assault, was banished to a deserted island by a judge who followed the community's recommendation for addressing Frank's actions, and there learned to look within himself and to care for himself. The love of extended family and community members is a strong theme. The notion of looking within resonates with Ellen White's teaching about going within, going to the core of oneself.

Frank Brown gave the LCES permission to use segments of the video *The voyage of rediscovery,* which he produced, and talked with me about the value of life-experience stories. Our talk was recorded for the *Teacher's storytelling video.* In Grade 6 "The Frank Brown Story" is presented in more detail, and the lesson includes his video. The lesson reinforces responsibility for one's actions and introduces reasoning embedded in traditional forms of First Nations justice, which often works better than the penalties imposed by the court system.

Frank was approached by a Native American video producer to tell his story through this medium. Frank turned him down at first because he was uncomfortable with the idea but later agreed because of its educational benefit. However, he ensured that he would keep control of the video representation of his story because he felt accountable to his community to accurately reflect the seamless connection that he has to his community and because he felt strongly about First Nations people owning their stories and portraying them respectfully:

> You hear Elders say, "I want to share this [life story] with you so that you don't have to go through what I went through. I [agreed to have my story portrayed through video] under [the] condition that I would have a say of how my story be told because I'm accountable to my people, I look to use an analogy of taking a picture of a wave ... a wave is a part of an ocean and I'm just one wave, but one wave is a reflection of all the waves in the ocean because they are at the same height and the same width going across the ocean depending on the tides and wind. It was really important for me to be ... an accurate reflection of where I came from. Because I don't detach myself from my community and my responsibility to my people to represent not only myself, but my community accurately. (Quoted in Archibald 1994)

Alone on the island for eight months when he was a teenager, Frank learned to take responsibility for his basic physical survival (although some food was brought to him), to accept himself by acknowledging and then confronting his past, his self-pity, and his anger, and eventually to accept accomplishment with humility. Ten years later he was able to conceptualize the cycle of thinking and action that he underwent: identifying a problem, acknowledging it, confronting aspects of it, and working through the problem to gain a sense of accomplishment. When combined with reflection, this final phase can start the cycle anew. He also created a mask dance with these four phases and held a washing-off feast with his family and community to publicly share his learning. Frank sometimes conducts workshops for youth about the teachings of his life-experience story. He shares his story with compassion and with a desire to honour the value of cultural reciprocity:

> You just have to believe in yourself and always ask for help from the Creator and from people that are there to help ... That's why I'm sharing ... even though I was the little bugger that I was, there was somebody that cared for me. And they said this kid has potential, that's why I'm sharing ... it's my way of giving something back to my society, to society in general. Because there was compassion for me, I want to show compassion ... the stories are very important ... I don't want kids to go through what I went through, because [it] wasn't very nice. I would like them to have a better opportunity to think it through ... Being locked up is not fun, being alone isn't fun. (Quoted in Archibald 1994)

Frank Brown's life-experience story has become a teaching tool for him and now others. His way of making meaning from it can benefit youth because of the many lessons/teachings that it contains. Story, combined with mask dance, song, and a community witnessing feast, are contained in a video and now in a curriculum. These educational materials serve to document history and to present a lesson in traditional justice that is internal to Frank's community. Frank's story also shows the educational, historical, and social value of a life-experience story. The LCES curriculum staff developed some pedagogical approaches to help teachers and students – the majority of whom would lack the knowledge – begin to engage in story listening and to make story meaning from both traditional and life-experience stories.

Teaching through Story: Some Common Approaches

Throughout the unit lessons, specific teaching and learning activities are presented for each story. These activities reflect some traditional approaches described by Elders in previous chapters and also relate to justice concepts. However, some teaching activities can be used with any story and are called "common approaches" (LCES 1994a, "Story Guide," 38-39). These approaches include telling stories with no explanation, using a talking circle for discussion, role playing and having fun with the stories, and story repetition. Telling stories with no discussion is explained:

> When you have finished the first part of the story, tell the children that they will hear the rest of it later. Also tell them that you will not be discussing the story right away. Explain that in First Nations cultures, long ago, storytellers often told stories and the listeners would not ask questions or talk about the story. They would think about the story and what it meant to them. Often stories were told at night, and children would listen while they fell asleep. Some Elders say that [they] would think about the story in [their] dreams. So, you will be discussing it later when they have had time to think about it, and "sleep on it." (LCES 1994a, "Grade One Teacher's Guide," 71)

The talking-circle concept, used by many Indigenous peoples today and modified for a classroom context, is a cultural way to share individual perspectives and understandings of a story:

> A talking circle may be used to discuss aspects or to share individual understandings of the story. Sitting in a circle is symbolic of the notion that all are equal and that what is said is respected. Some [open-ended] questions may be asked [by the teacher] in relation to the concepts of the unit lesson, but the purpose of these questions is not to check comprehension. It is expected that children and adults may not understand all of a story. That is all right. With discussion and active engagement in the story's aspects, understandings may increase. (LCES 1994a, "Story Guide," 38)

Usually, Indigenous talking circles are for adults, and their discussions are kept confidential because they may share difficult emotional experiences and thoughts. In the LCES curriculum the talking circle is a time for students to share the meanings that they have drawn from the stories in response to a general question posed by the teacher.

Each lesson lists the type of questions the teacher can ask. They serve as guidelines for dialogue and are not to be adhered to pedantically. Throughout the grade levels lots of role playing is recommended. Traditionally, some stories were theatrically presented at large gatherings, perhaps in a longhouse, and often song and dance accompanied the stories. Empathy with the characters and their situations, which enables one to relate personally to stories, is facilitated through various forms of role play. Sometimes, the teacher directs the role play, other times the students choose parts to act out, and in later grades they collectively write scripted role plays as a continuation of a story.

Repeating a Story

Many of the stories are used with more than one grade level. The concepts for these stories are sequentially developed so that the students gain an increased understanding of a concept, such as responsibility, over a few grade levels.

> This story ["The Creator and the Flea"] is part of the Law of the Universe, a much longer story. In stories, the place of beginning can change, depending on the purpose of the story. A story never really ends. Flea had to know all of himself, to know he had a part to play. That is a Law of the Universe. (LCES 1994a, "Kindergarten Teacher's Guide," 68)

Ellen White's story "The Creator and the Flea"[5] exemplifies learning by story repetition.

THE CREATOR AND THE FLEA

> The Creator was so great, he was a very special person.
> He could take a human form, with long flowing hair and
> holding a long staff. He had five souls. If he was needed
> somewhere else, all he had to do was clutch his chest and
> bring his right hand forward, and there in his hand would
> be a soft little ball of fluff, like feathers, and he would blow
> it away. That was his extra soul, so he could appear when-
> ever he was needed.
>   This one time he was attending a gathering in the hills
> with all his other people, but they were animals. The larger

animals were helping the smaller ones. And they were going to gather food for the coming event, for everyone who needed food.

While he was speaking, turning his head about, he heard crying: "Huh, huh," and whimpering: "Sob, sob." It was sad, very very sad. It was his right ear that was hearing it. For you see, his two ears could hear different things. His right ear could tune into things a long way away, good for long distance hearing. His left ear heard things up real close. So he turned a little bit to tune his right ear in. Very clearly there he heard that very sad sobbing, just so sad.

So he said, "I am still needed here, but I must appear there also, where the sadness comes from." And he clutched his chest, and he drew his hand out, and he blew, and there was this little fluff. It was gone, reappearing miles away on the hillside, and there was water way down below.

And all these animals were running. They were going hunting for food for the evening meal. The larger ones were helping the smaller ones, the smaller ones begging for rides, and the bigger ones saying, "Come ride on my back. I am big enough. Come little brother, little sister." The bigger ones were directing their little brothers and sisters, the animals that were going into the water, such as seal, lady seal and otter. Otter was very good at diving deep for the sea urchins. Some were going for the mussels that clung to the rocks and were bringing them up. If any little pieces broke they would eat them, yes, they cannot waste any. But all the rest of the food they gathered was taken to the gathering place, where it was all shared out equally. Some animals brought along roots that they had dug for their vegetables, and some were getting meat.

The Creator was very happy to find that they were all still using one common sound, one dialect, one language, you might say, and yet they were also using the unsounded communication. They were looking at each other and sending messages to each other through the air. And the air was so smart, it carried their thoughts from one brain to another. They were nodding, laughing, talking, but these little white lights of communication were travelling and flashing back and forth.

But when the Creator turned around a little bit, and tuned in the sadness, it came in very, very clearly, very close to him: "Sob, sob, hhh-sob, sob." So he followed the sound, and when he got there, he saw Snail Lady sitting there in front of this pitiful sight.

Snail Lady was saying, "Oh, my dear brother, I love you so very much. I am big enough. I want to carry you. Why don't you get on my back?" She was talking to this pitiful little Flea.

He was so small, but he was dragging these little legs. He replied, in a scared, sorry little voice, "Stay away from me! Don't you come close to me. Every time you come close to me, your slime gets all over these things I am dragging, just look at them. And look at my feet! They are bleeding again, and the bones are showing."

But he was touching his knees. He thought they were his feet. It was his knees that were bleeding and the bones were actually sticking out. Those long things he was carrying along on the ground were his legs, and his feet. But he wasn't using them. He didn't know they belonged to him, and he said, "I even tried to get rid of them, but I can't." The poor thing just kept dragging these things along.

The Creator went closer to Snail Lady and Flea and said, "Oh my son, what have I done, what haven't I done?" looking straight at little Flea. "We must try and work together so that you can become whole. My son, you don't know all of you."

But little Flea squealed, "I know me, but who are they?" he said, looking at his legs and feet. The Creator said, "That's all right, my son. We will learn as we go along, we will learn. Each part of you belongs to one side. And all the parts when put together are yours."

Very gently the Creator sent Snail Lady away saying, "Go follow the others, my daughter. Tell them your little brother will be there with them soon."

But Flea replied, "Oh no, I will not. I am going to stay here. I want to die, that is what I want to do. I want to stay here and die." So he looked at the Creator and whined, "You say you are my father, but you are just standing there.

Why don't you take me to that water, and hold me under until I am dead, because I want to die!" And he kept repeating, "I want to die, I want to die!"

But the Creator stood firm, and clearly told Flea, "My son, I don't take life, I create life. I help life be whole. We must start now. We'll start by doing something about your voice. We'll use that bush over there."

And in a pitiful little voice, Flea asked, "What's wrong with my voice? This is the way I speak all the time. There's nothing wrong with it!"

"No, my son," said the Creator, "that's your feeling 'poor me' voice, your 'I want to die' voice, that's what it is. And your eyes, they need working on too."

"These are my eyes," complained Flea. "They're all right. I can see."

"No, those are your crying eyes. You have cried so much, that you can't see as well as you could."

Flea looked up at the Creator, who looked so large to him. "You keep calling me your son, and you're not my father. You're too big and ugly. If I had a father, he wouldn't look like you."

And the Creator said to him, "I am your father, from far away. I am the father that helps to build, and I bring the message of the Universe that you are going to be very, very strong, and you are going to be a teacher to others. Now, crawl over to that bush, and pick some of the little buds and leaves. Chew on them and you'll rub the good juices on your eyes."

So Flea started to crawl over to the bush. Then he stopped. "Why don't you get it for me? You're just standing over there ordering me about. What are you good for anyway?"

"If I got them, then it would be for me. But it isn't for me, my son, it is for you." [end of first part of story]

So Flea crawled over there, dragging those long legs, talking to himself saying, "Now he comes here ordering me, telling me to go over here, and here I am. I'm just dying. Why doesn't he do it?" He's chattering and thinking all the way over.

But the Creator knows everything little Flea is thinking about. When Flea got to the bush, he picked buds and leaves and began chewing. Suddenly, the saliva liquid in his mouth started flowing because of the saltiness and bitterness of the little bush. Then, just as the Creator told him, he chewed a little bit and spat the juices into his hands. Then he rubbed his hands over his eyes, and his eyes started feeling instantly so much better.

"Now, my son," said the Creator, "put some in your ears." Flea had as much pus in his ears as he had in his eyes. It was just dripping from all the sand, and everything going in there and infecting it. And all the wetness from his crying had gone into his little ears. So he put some of the medicine in there, and in a moment his ears felt better.

"Father, it feels better."

"That is good, my son. We have to work together. We don't want to stop the good energy flowing now, we won't break it. Now rub your hands together." And little Flea rubbed and rubbed his hands together, up and down, around and around, until his hands were sparkling with energy. "Now," said the Creator, "go over to that plantain and carefully pick some." So, still talking to himself, complaining, Flea dragged himself over. He picked some plantain, but he even moaned about that poor plant.

"Look at this thing! It's so ugly and dirty, and all covered in sand and everything, bugs crawling ... "

"Shake it then, shake it well."

So Flea did that, and surprise, off dropped the sand, and even the bugs scattered away. Then he put the whole plant in his mouth, so much that his little cheeks were just puffed out. And he chewed and chewed again, swallowing some. But he had a lot of juice in his mouth.

"Spit it on your hands now," suggested the Creator. So all this mangled pulp-like mush, he spat it on his hands and rubbed and rubbed.

"Put it on your bones. Those are your little knees, not your feet. Those long things you've been dragging are your legs. Way over there are your feet. Because you are so small, if you used them the way they are meant to be used, you would be hopping up and down, up and down, and you'd never be left behind. You'd be gone with your relatives."

So Flea started chewing, spat it on his hands, both little hands equally, and he started rubbing that plantain medicine on his sore knees. And it felt sooo good.

"It's stopped bleeding!" he exclaimed. His voice was already so much better, and stronger. "Father, look! The blood has stopped! It looks so good now!"

Next the Creator said, "I want you to speak to them, my son. Yes, those are your legs. Stick them straight out and way over there." So the Flea sat up with his legs stretched straight out on the ground. "Now close your eyes, and look at them. Look at them!"

"I can't even see them."

"You will," said the Creator. "You will, when you really want to."

Then Flea started to get to know his little feet. He looked at his knees, then his legs, looking all the way down to his little feet. He started to get to know them. He touched his heels and his little toes and he could feel them. "I can feel them, Father, I can feel them." He got really excited.

"Good, so speak to them."

Flea kept rubbing his legs, and then his knees and hands, making more and more energy. He opened his eyes and started to speak to his feet. "I want you to be so strong. I want you to hold me up. Please, hold me up. I don't want to be crawling all the time. I want to walk. Be part of me, please, be part of me." So he tried to stand up and he could all right, but after just a little while a-toppling over he goes. "I can't do it, Father," Flea whispered.

"You will," came back the reply.

"But I can feel my legs, I can," said Flea, "and my feet too."

"Yes, my son," said the Creator softly. "Try it again. I think you're not speaking to them quite right."

So Flea started again, energizing all the time. "I want you to be a part of me. Please, be part of me." He really spoke clearly to his feet and legs. Then all of a sudden, with real energy he sang out, "Not just part of me, Father, me, all of me, me, me, me!"

And the instant he said that, it brought him back to the
beginning, when the Creator had said, "You don't know all
of you." But now Flea was whole, just like he had completed
a whole circle of discovering himself. He was whole now.
He jumped up. "I am me, Father, me, I am all of me." And
he jumped up and started to bounce. "Thank you, Father,
thank you." Flea was so grateful.

Ellen White agreed to lend her story "The Creator and the Flea" to the
LCES for use as a foundational story in order to introduce and begin
developing the cultural concept of holism by teaching students about
aspects of the physical realm. She retains copyright to this story. Ellen
told this story during a discussion with the curriculum staff and gave
direction for the type of teaching to be developed in the lessons: "The
story tells us to connect with ourselves, to challenge ourselves, to love
ourselves, and to understand every part of our body. In this way, the
body will return this love" (quoted in Archibald 1994).

The story "The Creator and the Flea" is used in four grade levels:
kindergarten and Grades 1, 2, and 4. In kindergarten the story begins
a unit and is told in segments over two lessons. Other stories that are
lengthy are also told in segments over two or more lessons. A number
of storytellers have mentioned that they heard stories told in this manner when they were young children. Often the segments seemed like
short stories.

The story activities, which include guided discussion, rhyme, role play,
and drawing/painting, take a total of six lessons to complete. Through
the character of Flea, the children are guided to learn about, take care
of, and appreciate the physical self. Individual responsibility for one's
own learning is then reinforced as the main story teaching for Grade 1.
Similar types of teaching activities introduced in kindergarten are used
in this grade level and completed in four lessons. The students also
share "self-discoveries" about the physical things that they couldn't do
in kindergarten but are now able to do in Grade 1. They participate
more with storytelling by joining in the telling of the story with the
teacher. In Grade 2 the story is "used as a basis for making 'Me Dolls' ...
They will 'put themselves together,' just as Flea does in the story. With
this activity, the students will get to know the important functions of
their body parts, and will create someone [themselves] 'worthy of care
and respect'" (Law Courts Education Society 1994a, 86). The students
are guided through discussion to suggest ways that they can take care of

their bodies, their selves, so that they are healthy and safe. In the third lesson their thinking is extended to examine interrelationships with caregivers in their lives. The Creator and the Snail are used as examples of caregivers to the Flea. In Grade 4 the concept of taking responsibility for oneself is again repeated through the story and used to examine ownership of one's feelings and actions. The story is a bridge to introducing conflict resolution. Imagery exercises, guided discussion, and role play are the teaching activities for two lessons.

The story pedagogy suggested in the LCES elementary school curriculum is at an introductory level. The premise that the curriculum staff worked with was that the teachers and students know nothing or very little about story listening and making story meaning. The curriculum developers tried to incorporate traditional aspects of storywork, such as learning in segments, in order to allow opportunity for the listener to make her/his own meaning and to have fun with story. The aim was also to provide opportunities for the listener to engage in the story through role play and with the story through discussion.

Applying Storywork to Adults
Even though these stories were used for learning with young children, they can have application for teenagers and adults. One of the curriculum staff members talked of her deeply felt reflections related to understandings about holism/wellness, personal responsibility, self-respect, patience, and personal empowerment gained from the story "The Creator and the Flea":

> "The Creator and the Flea" is a wonderful healing story, it's very much needed everywhere. When I first heard it – I was able to relate to some of it, [but] it was my second contact [when] I heard Ellen give the story at [the University of British Columbia]. Boy oh boy, it ... really touched my heart ... I said to myself, will I ever be that Flea? Throughout the project I was the Flea learning about myself working with people ... that story is like my guidance, maybe my philosophy in life right now because I very much believe that there is a Creator out there ... [I'm] working towards becoming whole, it takes time, it won't be just overnight, but there are other things that I also have to work through, and those are some of the healing things.

> I feel that anyone can relate to this story at whatever stage of life they're at. I feel that there is a common thread for everyone to [find] in this story ... whether it's healing ... or a hardship they've gone through,

or even the joy of accomplishing something in life ... Whatever we're going through, we value afterwards, so you come away as a stronger person ... [This story] could be an outline for your life ... for me it's one of overcoming obstacles, being my own worst enemy ... like the Flea was his own worst enemy. But overcoming that and feeling good, is like empowerment. I also felt that the Creator and the Flea gave me ... a vision in life, [where] you also have to have good thoughts, have good relationships, have good experiences in life because those are the things that are going to keep you going. Not to dwell on the negative things because that's what the Flea was doing and the poor Flea was killing himself and he would have died. (Transcript, 3 July 1995)

Some traditional stories have such a powerful impact on people that they become a philosophical guide for change; those who are ready unfold story meanings in relation to their personal lives. As noted in the example above, sometimes the traditional story becomes part of one's life-experience story, to be shared with others when appropriate.

Ellen White's most recent book, *Legends and teachings of Xeel's, the Creator,* contains stories for high school students and adults that are intended to help them "address issues that arise at different stages of their lives" (2006, 9). Ellen felt that teens and adults lacked Indigenous stories suited to their identity needs and life transitions. She also felt that readers of her stories needed to have some additional information that would help them to make story meaning. She worked with her daughter Vicki to develop supplementary texts to accompany each story. These texts, which are written as though Ellen is speaking to the reader/listener, relate cultural teachings that will help them to make meaning from the stories. The following text exemplifies this approach for another story about the Creator/Xeel's and Flea:

This little story is about life, death, and survival. It is the tale of the flea mother's journey from despair to success ... The flea mother hadn't listened to Xeel's very well in the past because she was a very critical person – critical of him, and perhaps also of herself. She had not been open to his teachings. But now, walking along the beach and feeling small and helpless, she was able to remember something from the lessons of long ago ... As the flea lady made her connection to the spirit, she stopped crying. She stopped thinking about how sad she was and how pitiful her son was. She decided to be strong because Xeel's was with her and she was not going to waste time feeling sorry for herself. She moved from self-absorption and self-pity to thinking about a solution – from inaction to action. (19-20)

Giving Back

Storytelling honours and respects the individual and the group. Many Elders teach that one should not simply accept the outward meaning of a story as an absolute given. A story often has many levels of meaning to it that are revealed to the listener at different stages of life, when the time is right. (LCES 1994a, "Story Guide," 40)

The curriculum developers, First Nations storytellers, and educators who worked together to complete the First Nations Journeys of Justice curriculum talked about the cultural principles of respect, responsibility, reciprocity, and reverence in relation to how they thought and felt about stories and how they approached their tasks of storywork. The distinctiveness of each principle fades somewhat as each interrelates with another. At other times their differences create a beautiful synergy, and they take on a distinct form – like a design on a cedar basket.

The principle of respectful relationships was developed and carried out by the Law Courts Education Society's curriculum staff in consultation with the Native Advisory and Teachers' Advisory Committees. Respect was shown in a number of ways: (1) the curriculum staff either worked with local community liaison people to contact storytellers or, when more appropriate, asked storytellers directly to participate in the project; (2) the curriculum staff then travelled to the home territories of the storytellers to tape-record stories and conversations and to ask advice about the contextual use of their stories; (3) the storytellers whose stories were selected were each given a written transcript, a copy of the taped session, and a draft copy of the story and accompanying lesson to edit as each wished; and (4) the storytellers approved the printed texts of the stories and retained copyright to their stories. They were also given opportunities to withdraw their stories. Storytellers also demonstrated respect for the curriculum staff and for the children who will be exposed to their stories by sharing cultural knowledge to enhance meaning and by carefully presenting each story in a manner appropriate to the intended children's level of understanding. Practising respect in this way is also a cultural responsibility.

Responsibility included ensuring accuracy of content and cultural appropriateness of pedagogy. Some traditional story approaches to learning, such as contextual listening, purposeful repetition, presenting stories in segments, and allowing story meaning to arise from individual thinking and connection, were developed throughout the unit lessons. Consistently following through with the ethical processes described earlier was a constant challenge. The large numbers of people involved, geographical diversity, time limitations, and cultural differences created various problems. The community storytellers also took on traditional teaching responsibilities toward their stories, which meant that the curriculum staff had to be sensitive and responsive to their directions.

Storytellers showed reverence through prayer, songs, and the ethical ways that they approached the work with the curriculum staff. Prayer or song helps to create a meeting place for the heart, mind, body, and spirit to interact. Silence creates a respectful space for reverence.

Practising respect and responsibility in relationships with people and toward storywork led to a traditional concept of reciprocity. Within many Indigenous cultures, one is taught to pass on what she/he has learned to those who are interested. This passing on of knowledge is a way of perpetuating it. Those who worked with the LCES group did so because they felt responsible for keeping their stories alive for future generations.

A major issue regarding reciprocity is that changes to cultural ways of making meaning through story may have epistemological implications. Because learners may know nothing about Indigenous stories, a certain amount of explication regarding cultural context and the story is necessary. Where does one draw the line between explication to lessen confusion and disrespecting the story and learners by telling them what to think? Elder Tillie Guiterrez, of the Stó:lō Nation, said: "You are helping them [children] seek out meaning and reason that lies within all things, to sense their own power and to develop the will to do what is right. If a young person has a problem, often times the elder gives them a story. The story does not give them all the answers. It shows them the way" (LCES 1994a, "Teacher's Guide," 8).

The community storytellers tried to show the curriculum staff the way through their stories. I have tried to be respectful in the portrayal of the LCES's storywork experiences by documenting them accurately and in sufficient detail. I have emphasized the need to develop respectful relationships with Indigenous storytellers. These types of relationships often become friendships. Going out to the field to "talk story" takes time, patience, openness, and the will to keep talking with one another in order to learn how to engage in story listening and to make story meaning; none of this is unproblematic. It is hard work. The next chapter shares some storywork teaching and learning approaches that result from the hard work of caring educators and storytellers. Coyote also drops in once more.

CHAPTER SIX

Storywork Pedagogy

The complexity of planning and developing aspects of an Indigenous story-based curriculum was examined in the previous chapter. Implementing this type of curriculum presents educational challenges for the teacher and the Indigenous community, as shown by the two curriculum experiences recounted by Greg Sarris and Lorna Azak (now Mathias).[1] The teachers in these settings would have benefited from guidance and direction from a skilled storyteller/educator like Dr. Ellen White or if they had possessed an understanding of a storywork framework applicable to Indigenous students. Ellen's story teachings are shared in this chapter to serve as a summary of the storywork principles of respect, responsibility, reciprocity, reverence, holism, interrelatedness, and synergy. Storywork pedagogy is also highlighted.

Greg Sarris (1993), a Kasha Pomo Indian, tells a classroom story of a well-meaning non-Indian teacher, Molly Bishop, who tried to incorporate American Indian values into her teaching because a member of a reservation school board recommended it. Molly Bishop wanted to use culturally relevant materials and chose the story "Slug Woman" to use with her Indian students in kindergarten to Grade 8. She found this story in a printed pamphlet, produced by non-Indian educators working for a local Indian education centre. I summarize the story here.[2]

SLUG WOMAN

Slug Woman, a short, small, long-haired woman wanders
around carrying a baby basket adorned with abalone shells
in front of her body. No one is sure if there is a baby inside.
A young couple has a baby son. The young man leaves
home to go hunting, breaking an ancient law forbidding
young men to go out until after the fourth dawn following
the birth of a newborn. He does not believe in this tradition. He has an encounter with Slug Woman and ends up
in a hollow tree with her. He begins to feel afraid and tries
to escape. The young man runs away, but Slug Woman
runs as fast as he does. When he reaches home, he cannot
stay because Slug Woman says that he belongs to her now.
She brings the young man back to the hollow tree, where-
upon he becomes very sick and begins to burn inside. She
says: "When you don't believe ... these things happen to
you. This is why you can't go home." The young man dies.
    The baby son grows up and overhears a story about his
father. He tries to search for some clues about his father
and finds the hollow tree and an abalone shell from Slug
Woman's basket. The mother tells her son about his father's death and warns him, "Remember this well ... as the
sickness may be visited upon you when your wife has a
baby. Don't go wandering around in the woods and do like
your father did. Don't hunt deer, don't gather slugs, and
don't fish." The son believed this law and obeyed it. His
children grew up to be good. They had children who
obeyed the laws of the Indian way. The family lived at
Timer's Edge for many generations. (Summarized from
Sarris 1993, 181-83)

The teacher had a dismal response from the students after they read the
story, and in her telephone conversation with Greg Sarris she said: "Most
of the students hated the story ... We couldn't even discuss it." They
said: "There's no such thing as Slug Woman ... That's all devil worship
... I don't want to read about no savages ... It's just like a cartoon. Not
real. Something like Peanuts" (173).
    At first, Sarris recounts feeling anger toward the students for not re-
specting the oral tradition. But as he thought about their responses in

relation to their colonized cultural, historical, and institutional schooling contexts, he could understand their reactions. He questioned the textual story representation, which was very different from the oral accounts that he and these students heard within their community context. The language of the story was "flat" and told in a voice of an anonymous storyteller, very much like the language of basal readers: "The story was about them [the students' culture] in a way that was not them" (192). He also questioned the influence of the teacher's lack of cultural knowledge and her reading pedagogy, which gave her authority over the students. Sarris infers that the students may have been angry and were rebelling against her authority:

> Presented in the classroom context, the story tells the students what an Indian is (i.e., a person in a loincloth who eats slugs and has rules about the birth of babies and hunting) and that if they are not like this Indian they "will be punished." The story's authority is associated with Bishop, so perhaps in a variety of ways the students may have been challenging and denouncing Bishop at the same time they were masking their connections with Slug Woman. No, we won't obey you. No, we won't be savages. No, we know nothing about Slug Woman. And that was the end of Slug Woman in the classroom. That was the end of the Slug Woman story. (193)

Clearly, the students should not be blamed for their negative responses to (mis)perceived "culturally relevant" curriculum materials. Perhaps the students were silenced, or angered, or embarrassed, as were Sarris and I and countless other Aboriginal students when our cultures were presented by "outsider" authority figures in ways that were stereotypical or disrespectful or that embodied "others'" perceptions of "Indian." These students' responses indicate that we need to bring back storytelling in ways that respectfully and responsibly resonate with the cultural community of the students. For Sarris and his relatives, "Slug Woman" is an important story and is alive: "For my aunts and me the story about Slug Woman had significance. For us Slug Woman is alive. She is seen and talked about in the stories we tell to understand the events of our lives" (174). Perhaps the students in Molly Bishop's classroom also needed to understand how to let Slug Woman stories into their lives in a way similar to that of their older generations.

In contrast to this negative classroom experience regarding students' responses to an American Indian story, a British Columbian First Nations graduate student, Lorna Mathias, had positive results from a First Nations literature unit with her class of twenty-six Grade 5 Nisga'a First Nation students.[3] She was teaching this class while completing an education project for a master's degree. She used a variety of First Nations stories written by First Nations and non-First Nations authors. A local Nisga'a storyteller also came to her classroom to tell stories on one occasion. Students completed pre- and post-tests, wrote journal responses to the stories, and engaged in conventional learning activities such as completing language charts, class discussions, and producing artwork. The three main topics that guided chart and discussion activities were: "(1) Our ideas about the story, (2) What we learned, and (3) ... Illustrations" (1992, 37). The post-unit responses indicated that the students learned "lessons or morals of the stories, respect for animals, elders, and other people, and how some things came to be" (41). The students observed that a good orally told story is

- when the teller changes his voice in all different tones
- told with expression and action [twelve noted this]
- if he might change the story and see what we say
- if he says N'eesda [which means, "carry on we are listening"] and puts more detail in it
- if it sounds like it is real
- if the storyteller has lots of excitement and speaks loud. (44)

The students questioned the "realism" of supernatural elements in First Nations stories that were in written form (similar to Molly Bishop's class) more frequently than with orally told stories. Mathias suggests that hearing stories from a well-respected storyteller makes the orally told story more credible, more real, and that children in her class preferred the "natural and human factor of storytelling" (56). Her example reinforces the need to have local Indigenous storytellers in the classroom. Other preferred learning activities included listening to the teacher read stories, writing about the stories in their journals, and drawing story characters, the Nisga'a crests, and petroglyphs. In contrast, students didn't like vocabulary building exercises and dictionary work (45).

Lorna Mathias's concerns about the students' responses to First Nations stories centred on their unfamiliarity with making meaning from stories and on their lack of understanding that "stories in the oral tradition have different levels of meaning and purposes" (56). She admits that "this distinction, unfortunately, was not an extensive focus of this literature unit" (56). Upon reflection, Mathias recognizes her responsibility, as the teacher, to increase her own understanding both of the nature of First Nations stories, particularly Nisga'a stories, and of their purposes for teaching and learning. She also mentions the tensions that she experienced between mainstream schooling pedagogy and First Nations story approaches:

> I decided that I still have very much to learn about our stories, and that most importantly, our stories are very complex and cannot be treated lightly, and are perhaps not easy to teach with the same methods as most children's literature ... the challenge we face as teachers in the public school system, that of trying to maintain a balance between First Nations teaching methods, and methods that we are also constantly reminded to use by education authorities. I was reminded that the skills taught in basic reading lessons, when used in conjunction with First Nations stories, should not overpower the stories so that the skills become the important aspect of the lesson, rather than the teachings in the stories. (77)

Elder storytellers, like Ellen White, would have been helpful mentors to Lorna Mathias and Molly Bishop. Such mentors could have guided their understanding about the power of stories and helped them to learn cultural ways to make meaning from stories. Ellen's methods of learning stories and learning to go into the "core" of a story are valuable story teachings and involve an interrelated approach.

Learning Stories: An Interrelated Approach

In my talks with Ellen White, she reiterated the process not only of intimately knowing a story, including knowing its content, but also of interrelating with the story to make meaning. When Ellen was asked how she learned to tell stories, she recalled the use of repetition, how she had to repeat the story during food-gathering activities. This form of repetition is different from the "needless" repetition discussed by Frank Malloway, as presented in an earlier chapter. He talked about repeating words in one's speech to a gathering of people. Needless repetition, according to Frank, does not add clarity or strength to one's talk; it turns listeners off.

Ellen's use of story repetition is needed in order for one to fully know a story. The children in Ellen's experience told stories "back" to their teachers not only to master the content of the stories but also to show their understanding of them:

Well ... sometimes they were on that story for ... a whole tide ... It's a whole tide and every time we come in from digging clams, ... we are still on the same story. We tired of it and they would always say: "Okay, tell it to me back. If you can tell it to me back as clearly; if I can understand what you are saying ... then you know the story. If you don't, then it means that you don't have the understanding." (Transcript, 9 July 1993)

In Ellen's experience, drawing parts of a story created a link to the children's visualization and imagination skills. It was a beginning step to making meaning from stories:

They used to tell us to make a picture [and] ... a picture frame in our minds and see right in there ... That's traditional, we draw in the sand, Granny always used to draw in the sand ... they [the students] can visualize, [they] have a very keen imagination ... you [are] tickling the imagination. (Transcript, 25 October 1993)

In response to the question of how teachers can learn stories, Ellen recommends more than just reading and memorizing a story. She believes that teachers first need to get to know the story using the method described above and then get immersed in the story: "If they just read it, they're just going to read it from page one to page two ... without any input from them ... They [should] start to read it, read a page at a time and [come to know] the story and [visualize] it, look between the lines, and go into the story themselves." She gives an example of working with a teacher: "He had to learn how to go into the story. He had to let go of reading word by word. He had to draw a picture like that frame and do the whole sentence all at one time, instead of just going word by word" (transcript, 25 October 1993).

By requiring visualization, the storyteller is making the listener or learner use her/his imagination. "You're making them work ... to become one: [the] story and your thought and the visualization ... this is [the same as] the picture in the sand Granny used to draw. It was very important [for us to] see." In response to Ellen, the curriculum worker whom I was with said, "I've always thought when I work with stories and I try and tell teachers that the story isn't telling the children what to think or feel, but it's giving them the space to think and feel, I'm hearing you saying some of that." Ellen replied: "You're making them work for what they are doing" (transcript, 25 October 1993).

Ellen emphasizes, again in reference to teacher preparation, that the first phase is to go within oneself: "It's also the first phase of training or going inside your own self. It says, 'If you don't go inside your own self, you will never learn what you want to be learning ... you [must] open yourself and go inside and communicate with yourself" (transcript, 27 July 1993). To go within oneself, to acquire self-understandings, one (including storytellers and children) must become humble: "It's teaching the child then to be humble. To be humble is when you get right into the core of what you're trying to get across to them. That was part of the training of zeroing in. You have to be humble to get in there" (transcript, 25 October 1993). I have heard Elders from the Coast Salish Nations say that to be humble, one must practise respect and reverence.

Ellen also believes that it is important to coach the teacher – that is, to work with her/him individually – which is similar to her traditional training. Today, more than ever, teachers need traditionally trained storytellers to help guide them in how to learn stories and in how to use them with respectful pedagogy.

Teaching Children through Storywork: "We're going to lift all the little corners of it"

This is why I like this work that we're going to try and zero in to make them see, and have them know that if they visualize a lot, their inquisitiveness starts overworking, imaginations and stuff like that, because it's what Indian stories are – to awaken the imagination – to awaken the depth of your very soul. (Ellen White, transcript, 27 July 1993)

Ellen uses a blanket metaphor to symbolize time to think, talk, and make meaning from a story. The blanket is a signal to the students that they are going to go "within themselves" to think. She suggests telling the story a few times before having the children talk about it:

They have to know that one day we're going to ... look at it [the story]. We're going to lift all the little corners of it ... To bring in their interest [say] ... we're going to talk about the story. We're going to lift this end, and lift it and peek under there to see what is going on in there ... how about the crying underneath there [in reference to part of a story]. (Transcript, 27 July 1993)

If children need help to think about the story, questions may be of use. Ellen introduces another way of engaging children's imagination:

Always ask the students as we are going along, "Do you think this could be useful in our thoughts? Can we use some of it ... as it is? Does it expand our thinking? Does it expand our magical thoughts?" Because each and every one of us hunts magical[ly] all the time in our thoughts. (Transcript, 9 July 1993)

If a child's response seems wrong or way off track, Ellen says that it is all right to tell them that this is the case and then to get them on track. She uses the circle analogy: "You got them right in a circle like, and they don't usually stray" (transcript, 25 October 1993). The circle is the story context that creates a healthy atmosphere for interrelated and synergistic sharing of ideas and thinking.

In response to my question about how children can learn to make meaning from stories, Ellen's reply was similar to that of Vincent Stogan and Ann Lindley, who talked about giving the learners just enough to ensure understanding and to pique their curiosity to learn more. This is also a developmental approach. However, Ellen also introduces the issue of student vulnerability:

This is where we call it shallow stories. We go to the shallow stories and the stories that we can understand today ... We were dealing with something that could never possibly happen in our time. But yet it still has a very good teaching, that we can use for youth today. So we give them just enough of a block [of a story] to understand.

When you are young you are very vulnerable, when you are young you are very imaginative, you imagine things so much – you fantasize – and I think that's why the old people gave them just a short block of story at a time. (Transcript, 9 July 1993)

When Ellen talked about the vulnerability of children, I remembered hearing the Stó:lō Elders say the same thing when the Stó:lō Sitel curriculum team continually and unsuccessfully tried to get stories for a plant unit taught at the Grade 4 level. At first, they said that they could not remember any plant stories, and then much later they said that they could not give us any because the stories that had good plant teachings were not appropriate for children to hear. These stories were inappropriate because the Elders thought that the information and messages of the stories would harm children mentally, emotionally, or spiritually. To prepare students to listen to a story and to ease this issue of student vulnerability, Ellen first sang a song, and then she introduced the story to a summer youth group of senior high school students in the following way:

> Stories were very important to the Native people. Stories go back perhaps thousands of years ago. We always ask why were these stories made and what we received with, we had to be taught. It was the only way that the old people can teach us. The story we are about to hear is part of these stories that are told to little bit older people.
>
> Remember again, too, there are always explanations, the lecture, in the beginning of the story instead of at the end. And we say: "Why do they use animals?" ... They said, "If I was to mention a name and point at one of you I might be injuring you [and] the whole universe." (Transcript, 28 July 1993)

The following exchange between Ellen and me reinforces the responsibility of the storyteller/teacher to protect the children and to ensure that they can comprehend a story that is told to them:

> Ellen: I think that it is the teacher's business, shall we say, to really watch what, how much they give to the students. When we tell [a story] to little kids it is just one very small section ... It becomes a very light and short story ... They said: "You can't scare them."
>
>   There are times when I am going a little bit [further than I should] and I can always tell. I start to get choked or [feel] something in my throat ... That's the time to carry on in a different phase. You will know how to do that.
>
> Jo-ann: Because you pick up from the people that that is as far as you can go.
>
> Ellen: Right! As far as you are going to go. They said it is your body energy that is telling you that. Your trained body energy ... because if you keep carrying on you [would really] scare ... the student.
>
> Jo-ann: That makes the storyteller's job really important because they are really the teacher [and should not cause harm to the student].
>
> Ellen: Absolutely! (Transcript, 9 July 1993)

In one session Ellen also said: "The story was told in a way so that the story became a teacher" (transcript, 27 July 1993). Having the story take on the role of the teacher resonates with my learning about the power of some stories. They can help one to learn, heal, take action, and then reflect on this action. However, if these stories are learned within contexts where the principles of respect, responsibility, reciprocity, and reverence are not practised, then their power diminishes or goes "to sleep" until awakened by those who can use the story power appropriately. The importance of teaching the younger generation the "right" or "proper" way of First Nations storywork is echoed in Ellen's words:

> It isn't going to end and die at the student; this is what you're wishing for, you're hoping for. You're hoping that student is going to ... turn around and give it to somebody else, give it in a proper way, a proper phrase, proper instructions, and a proper way of embedding deep within their minds – how to do this – how to make that other person feel.
>
> It'll also feel that nothing of the ... power of this story is ... lost. Or else it's going to be just a story. The power of the story is gone if you are not teaching it the right way. It will be just a nice little story, like the white man calls a fairy tale, a myth, and that's all it's going to be. (Transcript, 27 July 1993)

Looking to Indigenous traditional principles helps preserve the cultural power of stories and ensures that story pedagogy is educationally sound and beneficial. Coyote has one more opportunity to learn this.

COYOTE TRANSFORMED

Coyote still has his mismatched eyes, and he is wandering around. He is still feeling sorry for himself. Coyote has not learned to work the two new eyes together. He is travelling alone, feeling so sorry for himself, moaning away, and inside his own thoughts. He is not watching where he is going. And he is coming to a steep canyon. He keeps walking – not watching where he is going, and steps over the edge. The canyon is so deep that when he hits the bottom, his body is splattered all over the canyon walls and ground.

A little while later, that Rabbit comes along and sees Coyote's pieces. Rabbit shakes his head and decides that he can help Coyote one more time. He jumps over Coyote's pieces four times and after the fourth time, Coyote becomes whole again. He thanks Rabbit for the help, and continues on his journey.

A version of this Interior Salish community story was told by Robert Matthew, of the Secwepemc Nation. Robert said that this story is a shorter retelling of a version that is much longer. He believes that adaptations are allowed with this type of community story because it does not belong to any particular family or specific community.

In talking about the power of story, Robert said: "The storyteller gives some 'cues' about elements of life, connection to land and community, to the story listener. If you're ready, you'll get it. If not, then it will be just a story" (personal communication). Another time, Robert told me that he thinks the Rabbit is like an Indian doctor, who uses culture to heal, to help make people healthy in a holistic way – spiritually, emotionally, physically, and intellectually.

Indigenous peoples' history of colonization has left many of our peoples and our cultures weak and fragmented. Cultural knowledge, traditions, and healing have lessened the detrimental effects of colonization. Cultural knowledge and traditions have also helped us to resist assimilation. I believe that Indigenous stories are at the core of our cultures. They have the power to make us think, feel, and be good human beings. They have the power to bring storied life back to us.

Thomas King writes that "contemporary Native literature abounds with characters who are crushed and broken by circumstances and disasters, but very few of them perish. Whatever the damage, contemporary characters, like their traditional trickster relations, rise from their own wreckage to begin again" (1987, 8). Contemporary Indigenous storytellers and Elder storytellers are like the rabbit helping Trickster and us to become whole again through the work of story. Janice Acoose reinforces this same point: "Many Indigenous writers maintain Trickster survives incredibly challenging experiences only to live and begin again. Just as the traditional Trickster culture hero/fixer-upper survived great odds, contemporary Indigenous writers [and storytellers] are writing [and telling] their cultures back into stability and thereby assuring survival" (1993, 39).

What happened to Coyote's eyes in his renewed transformation? At one time, listeners would not ask this question if they had traditional story teachings. They would know that another story would come their way if and when they needed to know some answer to this question. Story listeners would also know that only they can answer this question, and maybe they might realize that the question to be examined at this time is: "How can Coyote learn to use his eyes and make them work together?"

Lorna Mathias's reaction to the story about Coyote "coming back" shows the interrelated and synergistic process that unfolds between herself as the teacher/learner and the story. She does not ask what Coyote's eyes looked like. She is not constrained by trying to make literal meaning. She places herself in the story. The meaning that she makes also resonates with the principle of reciprocity:

> This story relates well to the feelings of many teachers who try to use First Nations literature, but when they realize how difficult it is, or realize that they may have approached it from the wrong angle, and who may begin to feel sorry for themselves, and wander around until they hit a wall and fall to pieces. What we need to remember is that there is a wise friend out there who will help us put things back into perspective, if we listen to what they have to say, and learn from it ... This story seemed so simple, yet so direct and profound ... What struck me the most was how truly personal a First Nations story can be ... a good story can reach into your heart, mind and soul, and really make you think hard about yourself in relationship to the world. (1992, 78-79)

The principles of respect, responsibility, reciprocity, reverence, holism, interrelatedness, and synergy helped me get to the "core" of making meaning with and through stories. These principles are a beginning theory of Stó:lō and Coast Salish storywork. I believe that these principles must be understood and practised if Stó:lō and perhaps other Indigenous stories are to be used meaningfully in an educational context.

I do not want to generalize this storywork theory to all Indigenous peoples. However, these principles may act as a catalyst for examining and developing other storywork theories. Simon Baker's teaching is applicable here: "Listen carefully to what is said. Keep whatever is useful, and let the words that you can't use go out the other ear" (personal communication, 1996). Coming to know and use Indigenous stories through storywork requires an intimate knowing that brings together heart, mind, body, and spirit. The teaching of Okanagan storyteller Elder Harry Robinson surfaces once again: to know a story you must "write it on your heart" (Wickwire and Robinson 1989, 28). Walter Lightning's

(1992) teaching about "compassionate mind" reminds me to "come back" to the traditional teachings of the storywork Elders one more time. There are still outstanding storywork issues that need to be discussed in order to realize a compassionate mind and to fully appreciate the seven storywork principles.

CHAPTER SEVEN

A Give-Away

To be an elder, you first have to be accepted, listened to, and not laughed at. You have to be a good speaker ... You always know where it's [knowledge] going to be in your memory, in your mind ... They always mention a basket. (Ellen White, quoted in LCES 1994a, 107)

In this final chapter I return to the teachings that the Elders helped me to understand through my own reflection on what they had to tell me. I share "back" and "give away" my learning using the metaphor of a storybasket. First, I return to ongoing issues that have to do with the ethical use of stories and story ownership. Indigenous storywork is not an easy process but is essential to educating the heart, mind, body, and spirit, which is what we mean by Indigenous education.

Establishing Ethical Principles

While working on the First Nations Journeys of Justice curriculum, the staff and advisory committees talked a lot about the ethics of working with First Nations storytellers. In British Columbia there are thirty-eight distinct First Nations language dialects and 273 bands, tribal councils, and other forms of governance (Ministry of Aboriginal Relations and Reconciliation 2005). Such large numbers made it essential to develop guiding principles for working respectfully and responsibly with each cultural community and storyteller. The curriculum team and sponsoring organization had to engage various issues in order to develop ethical principles for engaging in storywork.

Obtaining Permission to Enter a Cultural Territory

Among many First Nations a traditional practice of respect is to ask permission to enter someone's territory. This tradition is still practised to varying degrees and in contexts such as meetings and cultural gatherings. Through phone calls, letters, and personal visits, we requested the permission of the tribal council, cultural centre, or Aboriginal organization involved in education in each of the cultural territories that we entered.

Respecting Cultural Protocol

The curriculum staff were sensitive to the cultural protocols of each person with whom they worked. Some engaged in spiritual practice such as prayer before beginning the work. Sometimes, a community organization had a liaison responsibility with particular Elder storytellers and had formal procedures to follow, such as with the Stó:lō Coqualeetza Elders. The staff member had a number of discussions with the Coqualeetza staff before being allowed to talk to the Elders.

Sometimes, the staff member felt like she was being scrutinized in order to determine whether the request of the Law Courts Education Society of British Columbia (LCES) was appropriate for the Elders' group. The Coqualeetza staff do this because they get numerous requests from individuals for cultural information and participation in educational projects. This procedure is one way to screen out those who may be a mismatch with the purposes of the Elders' group. The Coqualeetza staff members get a feel for the sincerity and ethics of the person or organization making the request, but the Elders themselves ultimately decide on the scope of their involvement.

Handling Verification Responsibly

The verification guidelines that were established included giving a copy of the tape and transcript to the storytellers and confirming the story text and story lesson plan with them. Problems arose when the verification process was not consistently carried out. An Advisory Committee member pointed out errors in the cultural information contained in her nation's stories. If these stories had been printed with the errors, the Law Courts Education Society (LCES), as the sponsoring organization, would have been held responsible for publicly humiliating her First

Nations community. The LCES would have been obligated to make amends and to "pay" for the errors by hosting a feast/potlatch for this First Nations community. This type of traditional cultural restitution is practised in this committee member's community as a form of justice.

Concerns were also brought up by storytellers who said that some of the textual language of the stories was too "fancy" and changed the "tone" of the story. They felt that their stories had to have "plain language" and be open enough for "students [to] expand their minds ... and be creative" (LCES 1994b, meeting minutes, 24 June 1994). After this meeting the curriculum staff tried to ensure verification of the textual representation with each storyteller and asked her/him to show approval of the story's text by signing each page. Requesting that each page be signed may seem like an extreme measure, but the LCES wanted to respond to the concerns of the Advisory Committee members who felt strongly about having the storyteller and LCES be accountable for the accuracy of the story's textual representation. At times, the curriculum staff felt that asking for signed permission made some of the storytellers uncomfortable because they felt that they were signing away their rights to their stories. The need to develop trusting and respectful relationships was reinforced once more as well as the need to ensure sufficient time to complete the verification process.

Moving beyond Intellectual Property Rights through Reciprocity
Each storyteller retained copyright to her/his story. Each story was "loaned" to the Law Courts Education Society for this curriculum project. This principle was officially adopted at the 24 June 1994 meeting of the Native Advisory Committee and the Teacher's Advisory Committee (NACTAC) when Elder Dr. Ellen White brought a letter that she had written recommending that the storytellers retain copyright to their stories. She was concerned about protecting the cultural integrity of the stories and wanted to ensure that she would retain the responsibility for her stories through copyright. Until this meeting, we hadn't even thought about what is termed "intellectual property rights."

The Advisory Committee readily agreed that the First Nations storytellers should retain copyright to their stories. However, they felt that another way to culturally enable the use of the stories was also needed. The concept of lending the story for curriculum use resonated with members' cultural practices of giving others permission to use their stories, songs, and dances. As part of the permission process, one had the option to indicate the limitations of use: for example, for teaching purposes but not for publication. The owners or stewards of these stories also expect acknowledgment of their cultural property. This acknowledgment is based on respect for territorial origin and cultural protocol. The acknowledgement puts into action responsible and reverent use of cultural knowledge, resulting in the practice of cultural reciprocity. Returning to good cultural teachings helped once again to resolve an important matter.

Issues That Won't Go Away

There were other major issues that needed attention and proved to be more difficult to resolve. These included using published and archival stories, keeping the spirit of the story alive, and whether non-Indigenous teachers can tell Indigenous stories.

Using Published and Archival Stories

Many Indigenous communities have published their stories for educational use – in British Columbia alone these include the Stó:lō, Okanagan, Tsimshian, Coast Salish, and Shuswap.[1] The use of published material may alleviate some of the concern among teachers about the appropriation of Native stories and help to dispel the concern that there is no material available to use. Some stories were taken from printed sources, both archival and published, and with each story we sought permission from the authors and publishers. If Indigenous people were involved with the publication of the book, their level of participation was noted through authorship, copyright, or introductory remarks.

Other aspects of using stories already put on paper are more complex. Indigenous involvement does not fully guarantee inclusive or accurate representations. Within a culture, various perspectives exist about interpretations of history, cultural traditions, and practices. Often Aboriginal people say, "This is how I was taught by my [ancestor]" in order to signify the cultural authority of their knowledge and to imply that other ways of knowing also exist. Sometimes, errors occur and are not found until the curriculum is in published form. However, it is essential that First Nations have the power to direct the textual representation of their stories and their cultural knowledge. Storytellers who approach their work and story representation in other media with respect toward the story, with responsibility to share it accurately and appropriately, with the teachings of cultural reciprocity, and with reverence will provide others with quality storywork.

Archival material, especially stories written by outsider professionals such as linguists and anthropologists, raises concerns of misinterpretation and appropriation. After careful consideration, we chose to include some archival-source stories in order to "tickle" people's memories. Some of these stories spoke strongly about traditional concepts of justice. Many stories have been "put to sleep" in people's memories. Talking about stories and presenting text versions helped to reawaken some story memories. One of the storytellers, Beau Dick, found such a story about his ancestral name in a book. The story also told about the power of his name, of which he was not aware.

> Personally, I think that this is a really important story of the way my ancestor was. It's interesting because I found that story in a book. When I saw it, I was really excited about it because that's my name. After I read it, I went to my uncle and told him about it. He also remembered some things about the story of Ga'akstalas, but he couldn't remember the whole story. (LCES 1994a, "Grade Six Teacher's Guide," 147)

Educators and storytellers from Indigenous communities might work together to bring back to life particular stories that have been put to "sleep," lost from people's memories, or taken from them through colonization. I recall the Stó:lō Elders working for months to recover a particular story, "Mischievous Cubs." They had heard parts of the story in their childhood. The process of remembering was like weaving strands of a basket together. Some individuals remembered a part of the story and contributed that piece. Others reinforced segments of the story. Slowly and carefully, they wove these pieces together until a complete story emerged. The important point here is that they reconstructed this story from their memories and from their lived experiences of listening and working with stories. They demonstrated patience, perseverance, and collective good will in order to keep the story alive.

Keeping the Spirit of the Story Alive

Remembering, retelling, and reconstructing stories are not straightforward matters. Another prevailing issue is how to keep the power – the "spirit" – of a story alive. The impact of a story from oral performance, aural reception, and visual contact between teller and listener lessens when the story is transferred to the printed page. Some may feel that the life force of the story has disappeared. Establishing learning relationships with Elders and hearing them and other storytellers tell stories develops appreciation and reverence for the stories.

It is this type of reverence for Elders, for story, and for Aboriginal knowledge that creates the disappointment, but it also creates an opportunity to activate a story's life force. The Elders entrusted me with knowledge about storytelling, and they showed me the power of using storywork through their talks with me, which I also learned by doing educational work with story. As a contemporary Aboriginal educator and storyteller, I recognize the responsibility that I was given, and I must practise the reverence that Elders showed toward the work of storytelling. The echo of Elders saying "we do this for the children" is heard once more.

The persistent work of the Elders and members of Indigenous communities to keep Indigenous languages alive for the current and future generations reverberates in the echo noted above. Stelomethet, Dr. Ethel Gardner, of the Stó:lō Nation, also recognized the responsibility that she was given to contribute to the revitalization of an Indigenous language. In the Stó:lō community she worked closely with revivalists of the Halq'emeylem language to document their life-experience stories in her text "Tset hikwstexw te sqwelteltset, We hold our language high: The meaning of Halq'emeylem language renewal in the everyday lives of Stó:lō people." She notes that "the Halq'emeylem revivalists draw their inspiration from the fluent-speaking elders who contribute unconditionally to the revival effort; their greatest rewards are hearing the children speak, sing and pray in Halq'emeylem" (2002, iii). Gardner's important work describes the efforts of Stó:lō communities to develop speakers of the Halq'emeylem language who then teach this language in early-childhood education and in kindergarten through Grade 12 and who also develop interactive CD ROM programs and other forms of digital technology for language learning.

Another Indigenous scholar, Dr. Jane Smith, of the Gitxsan Nation in the upper Skeena Valley of north-western British Columbia, was also given the responsibility by her Elders to ensure the continuation of Gitxsan stories through documenting them in textual form in both English and Sim'algax (Gitxsan), which she did for her doctoral dissertation, "Placing Gitxsan stories in text: Returning the feathers, Guuxs mak'am mik'aax" (2004). She also weaves the "Gitxsan worldview, traditions, beliefs, perceptions, visions and struggles" (184) into the twenty-nine Gitxsan stories that she presents. Smith is also developing a curriculum for teachers of kindergarten to Grade 12 that is interwoven with Gitxsan traditional stories and songs, the Gitxsan and English languages, and Gitxsan cultural knowledge. She is a classroom teacher who works along with other teachers in the important endeavour of breathing life into Indigenous stories.

The critical questions remain of how to keep the story spirit alive and how to make it live on the printed page or through media such as video and digital technology. The written or multimedia representation of a story may keep it from being completely lost through the passage of time, but the story is not the same as when it is orally told. I remember the words of Stó:lō Elder Ann Lindley, who waits to "look" at the story listeners before deciding which story needs to be told. A story on the page or on the "screen" cannot replace the magic and power of the interpersonal interaction between the storyteller and listeners. People keep the spirit of a story alive by telling it to others and by interacting through and with the story. People interrelating with each other through story bring a story to life as they relate story meaning to their lives in holistic ways. A skilled storyteller recounting stories for listeners is the best way to keep the spirit of the stories alive.

Non-Indigenous Teachers Telling Indigenous Stories

Placing Indigenous stories in educational curricula poses another serious question. Aboriginal communities in British Columbia have local education authorities, and some have established committees that make decisions about methods to research and document cultural knowledge, which aspects of cultural knowledge are to be implemented in schooling, and which personnel will teach or develop curricula. Making these kinds of decisions is difficult and may be influenced by pressures from family and political groups or by decision makers' religious affiliations. Ultimately, the people in the communities know who has the knowledge and skills to tell and teach Indigenous stories in the schools.

But what is appropriate and who determines cultural appropriateness are questions that continue to surface. Should non-Native teachers tell Indigenous stories? If they should, then how can they do it ethically? These questions were partially answered during a follow-up impact study conducted in six British Columbia schools from 1997 to 2000.[2] I was one of the researchers who observed non-Native teachers using the First Nations Journeys of Justice curriculum and interviewed these teachers, students, and parents about their perceptions and experiences. The teachers had participated in professional-development sessions to prepare them for teaching the curriculum. The teachers' responses indicated that they felt comfortable reading the stories aloud, right from the teacher's guide. Unfortunately, I didn't observe teachers telling the stories, although I did see them using the story-learning activities. They were enthusiastic about the curriculum, and they used the learning approaches effectively. My positive response to teachers using the First Nations Journeys of Justice curriculum is in stark contrast to the experience of others.

Without basic cultural sensitivity among teachers, appropriation and disrespectful use of stories are more likely to occur. A few years ago I attended an educational conference workshop about a First Nations community's collaboration with a public school district to develop a teaching unit based on some of its stories. A non-Native teacher and a First Nations educator took turns sharing their teaching material and experiences. Their interaction and their story-based curriculum seemed to exemplify respectful story approaches. During the session, an enthusiastic non-Native woman rhetorically asked whether she could tell a First Nations story that she had heard recently. My fieldnotes record my gut-wrenching reaction.

> She didn't know anything about First Nations stories, but said she wanted to learn more. Actually, her way of telling the story was entertaining. But my stomach churned, listening to her, and watching her. What bothered me was that she didn't know any cultural protocol: Whose story was it? Who gave her permission to tell this story? What First Nations culture did this story come from? She reminded me of Coyote showing off some new found knowledge without understanding or respecting its significance. It seemed like her storytelling was more for her pleasure than for the benefit of others. She was appropriating this story! (16 February 1996)

If non-Native teachers and Indigenous teachers are to use and tell Indigenous stories, they must begin a cultural-sensitivity learning process that includes gaining knowledge about storytelling protocol and the nature of these stories. I include Indigenous teachers here because even though I am a First Nations storyteller, I do not know the cultural protocol of many other Indigenous cultures. This learning process must be guided by local Indigenous educators who also possess the appropriate cultural knowledge. Ideally, good Indigenous storytellers should be hired to tell stories and collaboratively work with the classroom teachers on story pedagogy. I use the term "good" here to mean that the individuals understand the cultural principles embedded in storytelling and know how to engage in meaningful storywork. Individuals with this expertise have authority to tell their First Nations stories. Non-Native people must recognize that they don't have this cultural authority, even though they may acquire the expertise. Using story curricula prepared by Indigenous people that not only have stories but also have a storywork framework is one way to lessen disrespect.

The First Nations Journeys of Justice curriculum is one attempt to reintroduce Indigenous oral traditions into schooling contexts with educational intentions that emphasize using imagination, addressing emotions, extending thinking beyond basic reading comprehension, and practising concepts of social justice learned from stories. None of the curriculum work was without challenges, and mistakes were made. However, we were fortunate to have wise Elder guides, and we respectfully followed their teachings and guidance. Our curriculum storywork is shared with you in the hope that there will be many Indigenous curricula for future generations.

Returning to the Dream

My dream, described in Chapter 1, of going to the Elders and discovering that I needed to learn how to listen in order to find out "what they said" has come to life for me through my research journey into the world of Indigenous storywork. I did not know at the time what they were telling me, but now I do. Some of the Elders to whom I went were people from the Stó:lō and Coast Salish Nations whom I knew; others I came to know. All of them I came to love and respect. A respectful, reciprocal, responsible, and reverent relationship was established with each Elder. Even though time and geography creates distance, the close relationship has remained intact. It is my responsibility to keep going back to the Elders, just as Greg Sarris did in his learning with Elder Mabel McKay. She was a Pomo basket weaver and medicine woman who wove baskets according to dreams that she had. Mabel McKay's relatives told Greg Sarris that she had told them that he would enter their lives:

Mabel said you would come here. Seven or ten years ago. A while ago. When you weren't around here. Before you knew us. She described you, told us you would come and to take you in. It was her prophecy, her Dream. That's why Anita and I looked at you so closely when we first met you. Is he the one? we asked each other. Then I asked Aunt Mabel and she said yes. (1994, 164)

Sarris then realized why Mabel kept telling him the same stories over and over again when he was preparing to write a book about her life story.

The interrelationship between Greg and Mabel created a synergy of story threads that became a basket:

> Things came together. It wasn't just her story she had wanted me to know. While trying to help her, while trying to trace her story, I traced my own. I had pretty much sensed this. But it was more than that even. It was a blessing, a miracle. Hers was a life that gave, a life only in the Dream. I had never known her any other way. How else could I write her book? How else but from the Dream, what I knew from her? Her story, the story, our story. Like the tiny basket in my shirt pocket, different threads, sedge and redbud, woven over one willow rod into a design that went round and round, endless. (164-65)

Before Mabel McKay passed away, Greg Sarris wanted to know why she had chosen him. Her reply reinforced the value of coming back in order to maintain a teaching-learning relationship: "'Why'd you do so much for me? Why me?' She looked me in the eye and said, plain as day, 'Because you kept coming back'" (165).

Mabel also directed Greg Sarris's learning in her own way, despite his initial need to use an approach based on academic themes, which she readily dismissed:

> Mabel, people want to know about things in your life in a way they can understand. You know, how you got to be who you are. There has to be a theme.
>
> "I don't know about no theme."
>
> I squirmed in my seat ... "A theme is a point that connects all the dots, ties up all the stories ..."
>
> "That's funny. Tying up all the stories. Why somebody want to do that?"
>
> "When you write a book there has to be a story or idea, a theme ..."
>
> "Well, theme I don't know nothing about. That's somebody else's rule. You just do the best way you know how. What you know from me." (5)

Sarris tells us what and how he learned from Mabel McKay. I have also learned to appreciate her way and not "somebody else's rule": "Don't ask me what it means the story ... Life will teach you about it in the way it teaches you about life" (1993, 194).

The experiences presented in this book have taught me more about life and more about myself. I have learned about making meaning through story from the experience of doing Indigenous story research and storywork. Each chapter contains stories, accounts of others' experiences, and traditional teachings, as well as my experiences, reflections, and understandings in relation to them. Indigenous storywork brings the heart, mind, body, and spirit together for quality education.

I resisted doing an expositive book summary of the seven storywork principles of respect, responsibility, reverence, reciprocity, holism, interrelatedness, and synergy. Each principle has a separateness that is like a long flat piece of cedar bark used for weaving a basket. As each piece is woven together, it may lose its separateness and become the in-between space that creates the background for a beautiful design. As the basket maker continues, she interweaves the pieces, transforming them into distinctive designs. In the Stó:lō and Coast Salish Nations, people used to know from the designs who had created the baskets. Each basket maker had designs that were her signature, and each design had symbolic meaning. The baskets themselves had specific functions such as storing items, serving as water and berry containers, and sometimes being used as cooking containers. I take Elder Ellen White's lead by using the metaphor of a basket, and I present a "storybasket" in which to place my research and educational storywork.

The storybasket that I, and maybe Coyote, have learned to make comes from living stories and making meaning from them based on interactions with others, particularly with Elders. My first storybasket, which started from my dream, is not perfect. There are flaws. The next one may be better because I have learned some storywork principles and methods that I didn't know when I started this one. I need to keep coming back to the Elders to learn more and to have them check my storywork weaving process in order to see whether I am doing it in the "right" way.

In Stó:lō tradition a basket maker gives her first basket away to someone who may find it useful. I give this storywork basket to you.

APPENDIX

The members of the Coqualeetza Elders' Council wrote this letter to indicate their approval of the work contained in Chapter 3.

The Coqualeetza Elders Group has been working with Jo-ann Archibald since 1976. We have watched her go from a classroom teacher to working with NITEP (Native Indian Teacher Education Program) to getting her Masters Degree. Through all this, she never forgets about us. She still talks to us at our level. Whenever we need her advice with the curriculum, all we have to do is ask and she comes.

We would like to thank Jo-ann for checking things out with us before she writes them down. We think a lot of Jo-ann because she has shown great respect in getting the right information. She listens carefully with an open heart and an open mind. We thank Jo-ann for her hard work and hope that the knowledge she shares with others will also be treated with respect and honoured for the truth it is.

Our hands are lifted up to you Jo-ann. We are so proud of you and your work.

Coqualeetza Elders Council

Siyolewethet (Roy Point)
President

Siyamiya (Amelia Douglas)

Ann Lindley
Vice-President

Kwostelot (Pat Campo)

Kwethomet (Wilfred Charlie)

Skemcis (Mary Uslick)

On behalf of the Coqualeetza Elders Group   Oct. 30/96

NOTES

Chapter 1: The Journey Begins

1 The Stó:lō are part of the Upriver Halq'emeylem-speaking people. Halq'emeylem is one of three dialects of the Halkomelem language, which is also part of the larger Salishan-language family. "Twenty-three languages of this family span an area extending over southern British Columbia, Washington, northern Idaho, western Montana, and northwestern Oregon" (Gardner 2002, 8). The other two dialects of Halkomelem include: Hen'q'emi'nem, or Downriver Musqueam; and Hel'q'emi'nem, or Island version. The Halq'emeylem speakers in this book refer to Halq'emeylem as a language rather than a dialect.

2 For more information about the Stó:lō, see Carlson (2001).

3 This story is reprinted with permission from the *Journal of American Indian Education* (*JAIE*) using the same paragraphing format as in the original version. The *JAIE* is published by the Center for Indian Education, College Education, Arizona State University, Tempe, Arizona, 85287-1311. Despite the recent claims that challenge Terry Tafoya's Indigenous ancestry, this story has provided numerous people, including me, with important understandings that are not diminished by the aforementioned issues. As will be shown in later chapters, stories can take on a life of their own to become our teachers.

4 The Native Indian Teacher Education Program (NITEP) at the University of British Columbia began to conceptualize the holistic approach in 1989 using similar symbolism of the spiritual, emotional, physical, and intellectual as related to the circles of oneself, family, community, and nation.

5 See Archibald (1990), which contains a fuller discussion of First Nations orality and its relationship to forms of Western literacy.

6 Many Indigenous storytellers use literacy, and sometimes the quoted literature refers to them as "writers." Where the word "writer" appears in this chapter, it implies that the writer is also a storyteller.

7 Obviously, without the written text, I would not have learned as much as I did about First Nations orality. Another obvious point is that Indigenous people who are skilled in using the oral tradition can also be skilled with literacy.

8 See Battiste (2000, 192-202) for a discussion of cognitive imperialism in public schools.

Chapter 2: Coyote Searching for the Bone Needle

My work with the three Indigenous Elders noted in this chapter has also been published in my chapter "An Indigenous Storywork Methodology," in J. Gary Knowles and Ardra L. Cole, eds., *Handbook of the arts in qualitative research: Perspectives, Methodologies, Examples, and Issues* (Thousand Oaks, CA: Sage, 2007).

1 Over the years I have participated in various cultural ceremonies, written personal journal entries, engaged in quiet reflection, attended many storytelling events, given conference workshops and talks about storywork as I was learning it, paid attention to my dreams, and continued to visit the Elders – all of which was part of getting culturally ready and worthy in a holistic manner.

Chapter 3: Learning about Storywork from Stó:lō Elders

1 The Coqualeetza Complex was a residential school for First Nations children from 1886 to 1895 (Edmeston 1956). It was first operated by Methodist Missionaries and then run by the United Church. The complex became a hospital after the residential school closed.

2 The Coqualeetza Cultural Centre offers Halq'emeylem-language classes to two band schools and one pre-school in the Stó:lō Nation. The education office of the Stó:lō Nation also runs a Halq'emeylem-language program, Stó:lō Sxwali, which develops language curriculum and offers language training to adults. A language-teacher training program is also underway.

3 See Appendix, which contains a letter signed by the Coqualeetza Elders' Council approving of and supporting my research work with them.

4 Keith Basso (1996) gives examples of Western Apache stories that portray the important social/kinship link between historical stories given to place names. The Western Apache stories seem to give lessons about people who did not follow good teachings at particular places, and the place names and their stories remind people about respectful behaviour. When I read these stories, I first felt uncomfortable that the place names had negative meanings or feelings associated with them, but as I read more, another relationship between the land, story, and people surfaced. Basso quotes Apache Elders, such as Nick Thompson, who said, "The land ... looks after us. The land keeps badness away" (61). The stories associated with the land help people to keep the "badness" away. In contrast, those Stó:lō stories about X̱á:ls's transformations that gave places their names resulted from good actions, not bad.

5 Ann felt more comfortable not having the tape recorder on during our talks. She told me that I could use my memory and that she would tell me this story again if I did not get it all.

6 The term "oratory" in this section refers to the skills of one who is a designated cultural speaker for others at gatherings.

7 The tradition of men fulfilling the role of Spokesman is still practised at Stó:lō cultural gatherings today. Women also fulfil a variety of important roles at these gatherings. Women are called to be witnesses to events, such as a name-giving, at which they will speak. All gender roles are respected.

8 Earlier, I noted that people were taught to respect the speakers by listening and not talking to others when someone was speaking. Richard Malloway's example of people talking to others may seem like a sign of disrespect, and maybe it was,

but the important point here is that this was their way of giving a message to the speaker that they had heard, had gotten the speaker's message, and did not need to keep hearing the same words repeated in a needless fashion.

9 See Brown (2004) for a full examination of the importance of Indigenous emotional competency to learning and curricula.

Chapter 4: The Power of Stories to Educate the Heart

1 My story is a retelling of life experiences constructed from memory. It is interwoven with personal interpretations and contextual descriptions that resonate with the notions that the narrator can also be a commentator who offers "criticism" (Tedlock 1983, 236) and that "writing, as much as possible, should reflect oral tendencies to engage the larger world in which the spoken word lives" (Sarris 1993, 45). My story also resonates with ideas presented by Clandinin and Connelly (2000).

2 For a fuller description of the development and implementation phases of the Stó:lō Sitel curriculum, see Archibald (1995).

3 This story is not a traditional First Nations story. A friend sent me a written version of this story, but it did not have an author. I have adapted it and, over time and through repeated tellings, made it mine. I liked it when I first read it and began to use it for some talks in order to have listeners think about making space in their busy lives to hear the beauty of First Nations peoples' songs, words, and stories, which often get drowned out by the dominant society.

4 When I tell this story, I explain how I received it, and I say that it is not a traditional First Nations story.

Chapter 5: Storywork in Action

1 See *Delgamuukw v. A.G.: Reasons for judgment* (1991). This is the historic Gitxsan and Wet'suwet'en land-claims case brought to the Supreme Court of British Columbia. See also Ross (1992), in which the author, an assistant Crown attorney in northwestern Ontario, presents his experiences as a narrative about the differences between Ojibway and Cree concepts of justice and those of the court system.

2 For more discussion of the effects of the Indian Control of Indian Education policy, see Kirkness and Bowman (1992) and Battiste and Barman (1995).

3 The term "workable" is used here cautiously. The differences between Aboriginal concepts of justice and those used in the Canadian courts will not be resolved through this introductory curriculum for children.

4 I am grateful to the Law Courts Education Society of British Columbia for giving me permission to use extensive quotations from the storytelling video and the teachers' guides.

5 Some stories fall under a family's domain. Others know this and respect the family's cultural stewardship or ownership of the story. The family ensures that the story is taught to family members, and they have the responsibility to keep it "going." Ellen White's family gave her the responsibility to continue telling "The Creator and the Flea." Ellen White uses the publishing term "copyright" to show that she has cultural ownership of this story. I am grateful to Ellen White for giving me permission to use this story.

Chapter 6: Storywork Pedagogy

1 These two curriculum experiences will highlight some implications for curriculum and instruction about students' attitudes toward traditional stories and the tensions between mainstream schooling pedagogy and storywork pedagogy.

2 Sarris (1993) published the story in order to criticize the textual presentation as not being true to a Kasha Pomo way of telling Slug Woman stories, so the pamphlet's version is not presented in its entirety. It is unfortunate that the original version wasn't included in Sarris's book. A story summary is given here to introduce the story and to provide a context in which to place the discussion that follows.

3 The Nisga'a Nation is located in northern British Columbia, north of the city of Terrace. To date, the Nisga'a school district remains the only British Columbia school district run by a First Nations community.

Chapter 7: A Give-Away

1 For some of these sources, see Ministry of Education (2006). This guide, which lists many resources about Aboriginal peoples and cultures, was developed mainly by Aboriginal educators.

2 The three-year research study examined the impact of the First Nations Journeys of Justice curriculum on student knowledge, attitude, and behaviour. A mixed methodology of pre- and post-tests, qualitative interviews, observations, and journals was used. Measures of student knowledge and attitude showed improvement ranging from 13 to 18 percent. Students, parents, and teachers felt that the story component of the curriculum had a beneficial impact on students. The study was funded by the federal Ministry of Justice.

REFERENCES

Acoose, Janice. 1993. "Post Halfbreed: Indigenous writers as authors of their own realities." In Jeannette Armstrong, ed., *Looking at the words of our people: First Nations analysis of literature*, 27-44. Penticton, BC: Theytus Books.

Ahenakew, Freda, and H.C. Wolfart. 1992. *Our grandmothers' lives as told in their own words*. Saskatoon: Fifth House.

Akan, Linda. 1992. "Pimosatamowin sikaw kakeequaywin, Walking and talking: A Saulteaux Elder's view of Native education." *Canadian Journal of Native Education* 19, 2: 191-214.

Alexie, Sherman. 1995. *Reservation blues*. Berkeley, CA: Atlantic Monthly Press.

Allen, Paula Gunn. 1983. *Studies in American Indian literature: Critical essays and course designs*. New York: Modern Language Association of America.

–. 1986. *The sacred hoop*. Boston: Beacon Press.

–, ed. 1989. *Spider Woman's granddaughters: Traditional tales and contemporary writing by Native American women*. Boston: Beacon Press.

Archibald, Jo-ann. 1990. "Coyote's story about orality and literacy." *Canadian Journal of Native Education* 17, 2: 66-81.

–. 1992. "Editorial: Giving voice to our Ancestors." *Canadian Journal of Native Education* 19, 2: 141-44.

–. 1993. "Resistance to an unremitting process: Racism, curriculum and education in Western Canada." In J.A. Mangan, ed., *The imperial curriculum: Racial images and education in the British colonial experience*, 93-107. London: Routledge.

–. 1995. "To keep the fire going: The challenge for First Nations education." In Ratna Ghosh and Douglas Ray, eds., *Social change and education in Canada*, 3rd ed., 342-57. Toronto: Harcourt Brace.

–, producer. 1994. *Teacher's storytelling video*. VHS. Vancouver: Law Courts Education Society.

Armstrong, Jeannette, ed. 1993. *Looking at the words of our people: First Nations analysis of literature*. Penticton, BC: Theytus Books.

Ashworth, Mary. 1979. *The forces which shaped them: A history of the education of minority group children in B.C.* Vancouver: New Star Books.

Azak, Lorna. 1992. "Siwilaaka adaawak, Learning stories: A journey of learning begins." M.Ed. project, University of British Columbia.

Basso, Keith. 1996. *Wisdom sits in places: Landscape and language among the Western Apache*. Albuquerque: University of New Mexico Press.

Battiste, Marie. 2000. *Reclaiming Indigenous voice and vision*. Vancouver: UBC Press.

–, and Jean Barman, eds. 1995. *First Nations education in Canada: The circle unfolds*. Vancouver: UBC Press.

Bell, Rosa. 1993. "Journeys." In Linda Jaine, ed., *Residential schools: The stolen years*, 15-16. Saskatoon: University Extension Press, University of Saskatchewan.

Blaeser, Kimberly. 1993. "Native literature: Seeking a critical center." In Jeannette Armstrong, ed., *Looking at the words of our people: First Nations analysis of literature*, 51-62. Pentiction, BC: Theytus Books.

Bopp, Judie, Michael Bopp, Lee Brown, and Phil Lane. 1984. *The sacred tree: Reflections on Native American spirituality*. Lethbridge: Four Worlds Development Press.

Brown, Lee. 2004. "Making the classroom a healthy place: The development of affective competency in Aboriginal pedagogy." PhD diss., University of British Columbia.

Bruchac, Joseph. 1987. *Survival this way: Interviews with American Indian poets*. Tucson: University of Arizona Press.

Cajete, Gregory. 1994. *Look to the mountain: An ecology of Indigenous education*. Durango: Kivaki Press.

Calliou, Sharilyn. 1995. "Peacekeeping actions at home: A medicine wheel model for a peacekeeping pedagogy." In Marie Battiste and Jean Barman, eds., *First Nations education in Canada: The circle unfolds*, 47-72. Vancouver: UBC Press.

Campbell, Maria. 1973. *Halfbreed*. Toronto: McClelland and Steward.

–. 1995. *Stories of the Road Allowance People*. Penticton, BC: Theytus Books.

–, Doreen Jensen, Fedorick Asham, Quick-To-See Joy, Jaune Smith, Jeannette Armstrong, and Lee Maracle. 1992. *Give back: First Nations perspectives on cultural practice*. North Vancouver: Gallerie.

Cardinal, Douglas, and Jeannette Armstrong. 1991. *The Native creative process: A collaborative discourse*. Penticton, BC: Theytus Books.

Carlson, Keith, ed. 1997. *You are asked to witness: The Stó:lō in Canada's Pacific Coast history*. Chilliwack, BC: Stó:lō Heritage Trust.

–, ed. 2001. *A Sto:lo-Coast Salish historical atlas*. Vancouver: Douglas and McIntyre.

Castellano, Marlene Brant. 2000. "Updating Aboriginal traditions of knowledge." In George Sefa Dei, Budd Hall, and Dorothy Rosenberg, eds., *Indigenous knowledges in global contexts: Multiple readings of our world*, 21-36. Toronto: University of Toronto Press.

Chrisjohn, Roland, Sherri Young, and Michael Maraun. 1997. *The circle game: Shadows and substance in the Indian residential school experience in Canada*. Pentiction, BC: Theytus Books.

Clandinin, Jean, and Michael Connelly. 2000. *Narrative inquiry: Experience and story in qualitative research*. San Francisco: Jossey-Bass.

Clutesi, George. 1967. *Fables of the Tse-shaht people: Son of Raven, son of Deer*. Sidney, BC: Gray's Publishing.

–. 1969. *Potlatch*. Sidney, BC: Gray's Publishing.

–. 1990. *Stand tall, my son*. Victoria, BC: Newport Bay Publishing.

Cruikshank, Julie. 1981. "Legend and landscapes: Convergence of oral and scientific traditions in the Yukon Territory." *Arctic Anthropology* 18: 67-93.

–. 1990. "'Getting the words right': Perspectives on naming and places in Athapaskan oral history." *Arctic Anthropology* 27: 52-65.

–. 2005. *Do glaciers listen? Local knowledge, colonial encounters, and social imagination.* Vancouver: UBC Press.

–, Annie Sidney, Kitty Smith, and Annie Ned. 1990. *Life lived like a story: Life stories of three Yukon Native Elders.* Lincoln: University of Nebraska Press; Vancouver: UBC Press.

Cuthand, Beth. 1989. *Voices in the waterfall.* Vancouver: Lazara Press.

Dauenhauer, Nora Marks. 1986. "Tlingit Oratory." *Alaska Quarterly Review* 4, 3-4: 105-8.

–, and Richard Dauenhauer. 1990. *Haa tuwunaagu yis, for healing our spirit: Tlingit oratory.* Seattle: University of Washington Press.

–, Richard Dauenhauer, and Gary Holthaus. 1986. "Preface." In Nora Marks Dauenhauer, Richard Dauenhauer, and Gary Holthaus, eds., special issue, *Alaska Quarterly Review: Literature, criticism, philosophy* 4, 3-4: 10-12.

Delgamuukw v. A.G.: Reasons for judgment. 1991. 0843 Smithers Reg., 1-394.

Deloria, Vine, Jr. 1992. *God is red: A Native view of religion.* 2nd ed. Golden, CO: North American Press.

–. 1995. *Red earth, white lies: Native Americans and the myth of scientific fact.* New York: Scribner.

Edmeston, H. 1956. *The Coqualeetza story, 1886-1956.* Sardis, BC: n.p.

Egan, Kieran. 1987. "Literacy and the oral foundations of education." *Harvard Educational Review* 57, 4: 445-72.

–. 1988. *Primary understanding.* New York: Routledge.

Erdrich, Louise. 1988. *Tracks.* New York: Harper and Row.

Gardner, Ethel. 2002. "Tset hikwstexw te sqwelteltset, We hold our language high: The meaning of Halq'emeylem language renewal in the everyday lives of Stó:lō people." PhD diss., Simon Fraser University.

Goody, Jack. 1977. *The domestication of the savage mind.* London: Cambridge University Press.

Graveline, Fyre Jean. 1998. *Circle works: Transforming eurocentric consciousness.* Halifax: Fernwood Publishing.

Haig-Brown, Celia. 1988. *Resistance and renewal: Surviving the Indian residential school.* Vancouver: Tillacum Library.

–. 1992. "Choosing border work." *Canadian Journal of Native Education* 19, 1: 96-116.

–, and Jo-Ann Archibald. 1996. "Transforming First Nations research with respect and power." *Qualitative Studies in Education* 9, 3: 245-67.

Hamilton, A.C., and C.M. Sinclair. 1991. *Report of the Aboriginal justice inquiry of Manitoba.* Vol. 1: *The justice system and Aboriginal people.* Winnipeg: Queen's Printer.

Hammersley, Martyn. 1992. *What's wrong with ethnography? Methodological explorations.* London: Routledge.

–, and P. Atkinson. 1983. *Ethnography: Principles in practice.* London: Tavistock.

Hampton, Eber. 1995. "Towards a redefinition of Indian education." In Marie Battiste and Jean Barman, eds., *First Nations education in Canada: The circle unfolds*, 5-46. Vancouver: UBC Press.

Hanna, Darwin, and Mamie Henry. 1995. *Our tellings: Interior Salish stories of the Nlha7kapmx people.* Vancouver: UBC Press.

Havelock, Eric. 1963. *Preface to Plato.* Cambridge, MA: Harvard University Press.

–. 1986. *The Muse learns to write.* New Haven: Yale University Press.

Holmes, Leilani. 2000. "Heart knowledge, blood memory, and the voice of the land: Implications of research among Hawaiian Elders." In George Sefa Dei, Budd Hall, and Dorothy Rosenberg, eds., *Indigenous knowledges in global contexts: Multiple readings of our world*, 37-53. Toronto: University of Toronto Press.

Ing, Rosalyn. 2000. "Dealing with shame and unresolved trauma: Residential school and its impact on the 2nd and 3rd generation adults." PhD diss., University of British Columbia.

Jaine, Linda, ed. 1993. *Residential schools: The stolen years.* Saskatoon: University Extension Press, University of Saskatchewan.

Jensen, Doreen, and Cheryl Brooks, eds. 1991. *In celebration of our survival: The First Nations of British Columbia.* Vancouver: UBC Press.

Joe, Rita. 1996. *Songs of Rita Joe: Autobiography of a Mi'kmaq poet.* Charlottetown: Ragweed Press.

Johnston, Basil. 1990. "Summer holidays in Spanish." In Thomas King, ed., *All my relations: An anthology of contemporary Canadian fiction*, 201-10. Toronto: McClelland and Stewart.

Keeshig-Tobias, Lenore. 1990. "Stop stealing Native stories." *Globe and Mail*, 26 January.

King, Thomas. 1987. "Introduction: An anthology of Canadian Native fiction." In Thomas King, ed., *Canadian Fiction Magazine*, no. 60, 4-10. Toronto: Coach House.

–. 2003. *The truth about stories: A Native narrative.* Toronto: House of Anansi.

–, ed. 1990. *All my relations: An anthology of contemporary Canadian fiction.* Toronto: McClelland and Stewart.

Kirkness, Verna J. 1981. "Editorial: Struggles and triumphs." *Canadian Journal of Native Education* 18, 2: 109-10.

–, and Ray Barnhardt. 1991. "First Nations and higher education: The four R's – respect, relevance, reciprocity, responsibility." *Journal of American Indian Education* 30, 3: 1-15.

–, and Sheena Bowman. 1992. *First Nations schools: Triumphs and struggles.* Toronto: Canadian Education Association.

–, ed. 1994. *Khot-La-Cha: The autobiography of Chief Simon Baker.* Vancouver: Douglas and McIntyre.

Knockwood, Isabelle. 1992. *Out of the depths: The experiences of Mi'Kmaw children at the Indian residential school at Shubenacadie, Nova Scotia.* Lockeport: Roseway Publishing.

Law Courts Education Society (LCES). 1991. *Funding proposal: First Nations law courts education project.* Vancouver: Law Courts Education Society.

–. 1992-94. *Activity report: First Nations justice education project.* Vols. 1-4. Vancouver: Law Courts Education Society.

–. 1994a. *First Nations journeys of justice: A curriculum for kindergarten to grade seven.* Vancouver: Law Courts Education Society.

–. 1994b. "Minutes of Native Advisory Committee and Teachers' Advisory Committee." Unpublished meeting minutes, Law Courts Education Society, Vancouver, BC.

Lightning, Walter. 1992. "Compassionate mind: Implications of a text written by Elder Louis Sunchild." *Canadian Journal of Native Education* 19, 2: 215-53.

Lutz, Hartmut, ed. 1991. *Contemporary challenges: Conversations with contemporary Canadian Native writers.* Saskatoon: Fifth House.

Maracle, Lee. 1992. "Oratory: Coming to theory." In Lee Maracle, ed., *Give back: First Nations perspectives on cultural practice,* 85-92. North Vancouver: Gallerie.

Marcus, George, and Michael Fischer. 1986. *Anthropology as cultural critique: An experimental moment in the human sciences.* Chicago: University of Chicago Press.

Marsden, Dawn. 2004. "Expanding knowledge through dreaming, wampum and visual arts." *Pimatisiwin: A Journal of Aboriginal and Indigenous Community Health* 2, 2: 53-73.

Mathias, Lorna. *See* Azac, Lorna.

Medicine, Beatrice. 1987. "My elders tell me." In Jean Barman, Yvonne Hebert, and Don McCaskill, eds., *Indian education in Canada.* Vol. 2: *The challenge,* 142-52. Vancouver: UBC Press.

Milloy, John. 1999. *"A National Crime": The Canadian government and the residential school system, 1879 to 1986.* Manitoba: University of Manitoba Press.

Ministry of Aboriginal Relations and Reconciliation. 2005. *A guide to Aboriginal organizations and services in British Columbia, 2005-2006.* Victoria: BC Ministry of Aboriginal Relations and Reconciliation.

Ministry of Education. 2006. *Shared learnings: Integrating BC Aboriginal content K-10.* Victoria: BC Ministry of Education.

Mishler, Eisner. 1986. *Research interviewing: Context and narrative.* Cambridge, MA, and London: Harvard University Press.

Momaday, N. Scott. 1969. *The way to Rainy Mountain.* New Mexico: University of New Mexico Press.

Neel, David. 1992. *Our chiefs and elders: Words and photographs of Native leaders.* Vancouver: UBC Press.

Olson, David. 1987. "An introduction to understanding literacy." *Interchange* 18, 1-2: 1-8.

Ong, Walter. 1971. *Rhetoric, romance, and technology.* London: Cornell University Press.

–. 1982. *Orality and literacy.* London: Methuen.

Ortiz, Simon. 1992. *Woven stone.* Tucson: University of Arizona Press.

Pepper, Floy, and Steve Henry. 1991. "An Indian perspective of self-esteem." *Canadian Journal of Native Education* 18, 2: 145-60.

Pryce, Paula. 1992. "The manipulation of culture and history: A critique of two expert witnesses." *Native Studies Review* 8, 1: 35-46.

Ross, Rupert. 1992. *Dancing with a ghost: Exploring Indian reality.* Markham: Octopus.

Royal Commission on Aboriginal Peoples (RCAP). 1996a. *Report of the Royal Commission on Aboriginal Peoples.* Vol. 1, *Looking forward, looking back.* Ottawa: Canada Communication Group.

–. 1996b. *Report of the Royal Commission on Aboriginal Peoples*. Vol. 3: *Gathering strength*. Ottawa: Canada Communications Group.

Ruffo, Armand. 1993. "Inside looking out: Reading tracks from a Native perspective." In Jeannette Armstrong, ed., *Looking at the words of our people: First Nations analysis of literature*, 161-76. Penticton, BC: Theytus Books.

Sarris, Greg. 1993. *Keeping Slug Woman alive: A holistic approach to American Indian texts*. Berkeley, CA: University of California Press.

–. 1994. *Mabel McKay: Weaving the dream*. Berkeley, CA: University of California Press.

Scollon, Ron, and Suzanne Scollon. 1981. *Narrative, literacy and face in interethnic communication*. New Jersey: Ablex Publishing.

Silko, Leslie Marmon. 1981. *Storyteller*. New York: Seaver Books.

–. 1996. *Yellow Woman and a beauty of the spirit: Essays on Native American life today*. New York: Simon and Schuster.

Sioui, Georges. 1992. *For an Amerindian autohistory: An essay on the foundations of a social ethic*. Montreal and Kingston: McGill-Queen's University Press.

Smith, Graham Hingangaroa. 2000. "Protecting and respecting Indigenous knowledge." In Marie Battiste, ed., *Reclaiming Indigenous voice and vision*, 209-24. Vancouver: UBC Press.

Smith, Jane. 2004. "Placing Gitxsan stories in text: Returning the feathers, Guuxs mak'am mik'aax." PhD diss., University of British Columbia.

Smith, Linda Tuhiwai. 1999. *Decolonizing methodologies: Research and Indigenous peoples*. London: Zed Books.

Sterling, Shirley. 1992. *My name is Seepeetza*. Toronto: Groundwood.

–. 1997. "The grandmother stories: Oral tradition and the transmission of culture." PhD diss., University of British Columbia.

–. 2002. "Yetko and Sophie: Nlakapamux cultural professors." *Canadian Journal of Native Education* 26, 1: 4-10.

Tafoya, Terry. 1982. "Coyote's eyes: Native cognition styles." *Journal of American Indian Education* 22, 2: 21-33.

Tedlock, Dennis. 1983. *The spoken word and the work of interpretation*. Philadelphia: University of Pennsylvania Press.

Toelken, B., and T. Scott. 1981. "Poetic retranslation and the 'pretty languages' of Yellowman." In K. Kroeber, ed., *Traditional literatures of the American Indian: Texts and interpretations*, 65-116. Lincoln: University of Nebraska Press.

Urion, Carl. 1991. "Changing academic discourse about First Nations education: Using two pairs of eyes." *Canadian Journal of Native Education* 18, 1: 1-9.

Vizenor, Gerald. 1987. "Follow the trickroutes: An interview with Gerald Vizenor." In Joseph Bruchac, ed., *Survival this way: Interviews with American Indian poets*, 287-310. Tucson: University of Arizona Press.

Werner, Walter, B. Connors, Ted Aoki, and J. Dahlie. 1977. *Whose culture? Whose heritage? Ethnicity within Canadian social studies curricula*. Vancouver: Centre for the Study of Curriculum and Instruction, University of British Columbia.

White, Ellen. 1981. *Kwulasulwut: Stories from the Coast Salish*. New ed. Penticton, BC: Theytus Books.

–. 2006. *Legends and teachings of Xeel's, the Creator*. Vancouver: Pacific Educational Press.

–, and Jo-ann Archibald. 1992. "Kwulasulwut s yuth: Ellen White's teachings." *Canadian Journal of Native Education* 19, 2: 150-64.

Wickwire, Wendy. 1991. "On evaluating ethnographic representations: The case of the Okanagan of south central British Columbia." *Canadian Journal of Native Education* 18, 2: 233-44.

–. 1992. *Nature power: In the spirit of an Okanagan storyteller*. Vancouver: Douglas and McIntyre.

–, and H. Robinson. 1989. *Write it on your heart: The epic world of an Okanagan storyteller*. Vancouver: Talonbooks and Theytus Books.

Womack, Craig. 1999. *Red on red: Native American literary separatism*. Minneapolis: University of Minnesota Press.

Young-Ing, Greg. 1993. "Aboriginal peoples' estrangement: Marginalization in the publishing industry." In Jeannette Armstrong, ed., *Looking at the words of our people: First Nations analysis of literature*, 177-87. Penticton, BC: Theytus Books.

INDEX